HIROSHIMA

Also by Ronald Takaki

For Carol,
companion and collaborator

HIROSHIMA

WHY AMERICA DROPPED THE ATOMIC BOMB

RONALD TAKAKI

Little, Brown and Company

BOSTON   NEW YORK   TORONTO   LONDON

First American Edition

The author is grateful for permission to include the following previously published material: excerpt from *Dear Bess* by Robert H. Ferrell, copyright © 1983 by Robert H. Ferrell, reprinted by permission of W.W. Norton and Company; excerpts from "U.S. 1946 King's X" from *Complete Poems of Robert Frost* by Robert Frost, copyright 1949 by Robert Frost, reprinted by permission of Henry Holt and Company; excerpts from *I Was There* by William Leahy, copyright © 1950 by William Leahy, reprinted by permission of McGraw-Hill, Inc.; excerpts from *Plain Speaking* by Merle Miller, copyright © 1986 by Merle Miller, reprinted by permission of Berkley Publishing Group; excerpts from the Henry L. Stimson Papers, Manuscripts and Archives, reprinted by permission of Yale University Library; excerpt from *The Good War* by Studs Terkel, copyright © 1984 by Studs Terkel, reprinted by permission of Pantheon Books, a division of Random House, Inc.

Library of Congress Cataloging-in-Publication Data

Takaki, Ronald T.
    Hiroshima: why America dropped the atomic bomb/Ronald Takaki.
    — 1st American ed.
        p.   cm.
    ISBN 0-316-83124-7
    1. World War, 1939–1945 — United States.   2. Atomic bomb — United
States — History.   3. United States — Politics and
government — 1945–1953.   4. Strategy.   5. World War, 1939–1945 —
Campaigns — Japan.   6. Hiroshima-shi (Japan) — History — Bombardment,
1945.   I. Title.
D769.2.T35   1995
940.54'25 — dc20   95-13546

10   9   8   7   6   5   4   3   2   1

MV - NY

Published simultaneously in Canada
by Little, Brown & Company (Canada) Limited

Printed in the United States of America

CONTENTS

HIROSHIMA

HIROSHIMA

1

"A PAST THAT IS NOT EVEN PAST"

O brave new world . . .

MIRANDA

The cloud-capp'd towers, the gorgeous palaces,
The solemn temples, the great globe itself,
Yea, all which it inherit, shall dissolve
And, like this insubstantial pageant faded,
Leave not a rack behind.

PROSPERO

All torment, trouble, wonder and amazement
Inhabits here: some heavenly power guide us
Out of this fearful country!

GONZALO

William Shakespeare, *The Tempest*[1]

Hiroshima: Into a Fearful New World

Although General Douglas MacArthur was the supreme commander of Allied forces in the Pacific, he was not consulted
about whether to use the atomic bomb on Hiroshima. In fact,
he was informed of the decision only forty-eight hours before
the fateful flight of the *Enola Gay*.[2]

MacArthur considered the bomb "completely unnecessary"
from a military point of view: he believed that the Japanese were

practically defeated.[3] In July, when the general learned that Japan had asked Russia to negotiate a surrender with the United States, he told his staff: "This is it. The war is over. Hold everything in place for Olympic and Coronet [names for the invasion plans], but drop all work on them and get busy on the occupation." A member of MacArthur's staff in Manila, Horace A. Thompson, Jr., recalled: "We expected acceptance of the Japanese surrender daily, but on Aug. 5 we received word from Washington that all aircraft should stay out of the vicinity of Kyushu on Aug. 6." After the bomb was dropped on Hiroshima, he added, "Gen. MacArthur was livid."[4]

W. E. Rhoades, MacArthur's pilot during World War II, recalled seeing the general "depressed" immediately afterward. MacArthur seemed to be "in a daze." According to Rhoades, the supreme commander could see "a complete change in the whole structure of society and the way society was going in the future. Here was the turning point."[5]

A tremendously significant event had occurred. But General MacArthur did not fully understand *why* the United States had dropped the atomic bomb.

Recently, Lance Morrow of *Time* magazine offered an explanation. If we could travel backward in a "time machine," he wrote, we would understand that Hiroshima was destroyed by an atomic blast for an "excellent" reason. "Events occur in contexts," and in 1945, "it seemed that nothing less than such a devastation would serve to eradicate a Japanese militarist regime." Thus, the United States had dropped the atomic bomb on Hiroshima in order to end the war "almost instantly" and avoid a bloodly invasion, thereby saving both Japanese and American lives.[6]

Unfortunately, Morrow simply does not have the necessary facts. While we may never know everything, we now have more evidence on why the bomb was dropped. Today, we are able to examine crucial, recently declassified military documents, such as the June 15, 1945, report to the Joint Chiefs of Staff, the diaries of key advisers like Secretary of War Henry Stimson and Admiral William Leahy, memoirs of important policymakers like Secretary of State James Byrnes and Manhattan Project director Major General Leslie Groves, recollections and papers of military leaders like Dwight D. Eisenhower and Douglas MacArthur, and files of atomic scientists such as J. Robert Oppenheimer and Leo Szilard. More important, we have the papers of Harry Truman, including letters to his wife, sister, and mother, as well as his secret Potsdam diary, which was discovered in 1979, seven years after his death.[7]

These records have opened the way to a more comprehensive and accurate understanding of the reasons for the atomic attack. But how do we organize and interpret the information they reveal?

One way is to view the question of Hiroshima from different angles. In this historical drama, we can allow the actors, such as President Truman and Secretary of State Byrnes, to give their versions of what happened. However, we discover that sometimes the same individual gave different accounts of the same events, depending on when he told his story, and to whom. Often the stories were presented in letters written at the time the events were occurring. Once in a while, they were soliloquies, self-recordings made after the happenings of the day and handwritten in private diaries, such as those of Secretary of War Stimson and Truman.

Occasionally, the stories were recollections — such as Stimson's *Harper's* magazine article on why the bomb was dropped, Truman's *Memoirs*, Byrnes's *Speaking Frankly*, and General Groves's *Now It Can Be Told*. In most cases, these memoirs were written to explain the strategic decisions made by the authors and to educate future generations about what had happened.[8]

Some of the memoirs were written with historians in mind. In *I Was There: The Personal Story of the Chief of Staff to Presidents Roosevelt and Truman, Based on His Notes and Diaries Made at the Time,* Admiral Leahy wrote: "In the hope of being of some small aid to the historians who must fit together the vast jigsaw puzzle of war history, I have been persuaded to condense from these personal records an account of my part in handling some of the pieces of that puzzle."[9]

As we look at the pieces of our puzzle, reconfigure known evidence, consider recently released information, bring together diverse materials, such as military reports and love letters, and examine different versions of what happened, we find ourselves challenged to ponder an event that changed the course of history forever.

The Global Context of the Bomb

The decision to deploy the bomb was made within a larger context than just the war against Japan. The utter obliteration of Hiroshima on August 6, 1945, and then Nagasaki three days later did, in fact, bring the Pacific War to an end. But, as historians Gar Alperovitz and Martin Sherwin have amply documented, the decision was also related to postwar concerns — the reality of Soviet expansion in Eastern Europe as well as in Asia and, more important, the fearful prospect of an atomic arms race.[10]

When Truman suddenly became president in April of 1945, he knew that his main responsibility was to terminate the war. But another problem quickly became preoccupying. "My father's overriding concern in these first weeks," Truman's daughter, Margaret, noted, "was our policy toward Russia."[11] Truman's diary and memoirs clearly reveal that he was thinking more about Russia than Japan.

Some of the key policymakers around Truman were also worried about an emerging Russian threat. Secretary of War Stimson, Truman noted, was "at least as much concerned with the role of the atomic bomb in the shaping of history as in its capacity to shorten the war."[12] Shortly after the bombing of Hiroshima, on September 11, 1945, Stimson told Truman: "I consider the problem of our satisfactory relations with Russia as not merely connected but as virtually dominated by the problem of the atomic bomb."[13] Secretary of State Byrnes calculated that "our possessing and demonstrating the bomb would make Russia more manageable in Europe." He linked the atomic bombing of Japan to his strategy of containing the Soviet Union and frustrating Stalin's expansionist ambitions in Europe and Asia. "The demonstration of the bomb," Byrnes thought, "might impress Russia with America's military might."[14] As the key individual responsible for both the development of the new weapon and its deployment, Manhattan Project director Groves described the atomic bomb's larger purpose more directly: "There was never from about two weeks from the time I took charge of this Project any illusion on my part but that Russia was our enemy, and the Project was conducted on that basis."[15]

Intersecting this already volatile political situation was the reality of race in American culture. Ever since the first contact between the English settlers and the Powhatans in Virginia in 1607, and then the arrival of Africans in 1619, race has been significant in our history.[16] Hiroshima, as it turns out, was no exception.

Rooted in the nineteenth century, anti-Asian prejudice contributed to the way Americans quickly racialized the Pacific war. When the first Chinese immigrants arrived, they were condemned as the "yellow peril." Then came the Japanese immigrants. They, too, found themselves the targets of stereotyping, discrimination, violence, and exclusion that would lead directly to the internment camps of World War II.[17]

For the United States during the years between Japan's attack on Pearl Harbor and America's atomic bombing of Hiroshima, there were two wars — the European war and the Pacific war. In Europe, the enemy was identified as Hitler and the Nazis, not the German people. In the Pacific, on the other hand, American anger was generally aimed at an entire people — the "Japs." During the war, the Japanese were condemned as demons, a monkey race, savages, and beasts.

"We were very patriotic," recalled Peggy Terry in an interview with Studs Terkel, "and we understood that the Nazis were someone who would have to be stopped." In the movies, however, the Germans were portrayed as tall and handsome. "There'd be one meanie, a little short dumpy bad Nazi," she said. "But the main characters were good-lookin' and they looked like us." On the other hand, Terry noted, "with the Japanese, that was a whole different thing. We were just ready to wipe them out. They sure as heck didn't look like us. They were yellow little creatures that smiled when they bombed our boys."[18]

What intensified the racialized rage against the Japanese was the devastating surprise attack. Americans bitterly remembered Pearl Harbor. "Never before has the nation fought a war in which our troops so hate the enemy and want to kill him," *Newsweek* reported in January 1945. "This intense hatred was first aroused by the sneak attack on Pearl Harbor."[19]

Thus, the decision to drop the atomic bomb was made within a context of immense complexity. The military need to end the war, the political confrontation with Russia, and the cultural passions of rage crisscrossed dynamically.

"The Eye of the Storm": The Final Decision

In the making of the fateful decision, however, there was also the human dimension, or what C. Wright Mills termed the "sociological imagination" — the intersections of individuals with society.[20]

Truman and the policymakers around him made choices that greatly influenced the way the war ended. In his *Harper's* essay, Secretary of War Stimson cautioned: "No single individual can hope to know exactly what took place in the minds of all of those who had a share in these events. . . ."[21] But an effort must be made to learn what was in their minds. Personalities mattered, especially in the decision to drop the bomb.

As president and commander in chief of the armed forces, Truman made the decision and insisted that he alone was responsible. "The buck stops here," he always said.[22] In a 1948 letter to his sister, Mary, Truman wrote: "On that trip coming home [from Potsdam in July 1945] I ordered the Atomic Bomb to be dropped on Hiroshima and Nagasaki. It was a terrible decision. But I made it."[23] In his published memoirs, he again stated: "The final decision of where and when to use the atomic bomb was up to me. Let there be no mistake about it."[24]

After he ordered the atomic attack, Truman refused to question his action. The unwillingness to reflect on decisions once they had been made is often seen as an American characteristic. We tend to think of ourselves as constantly reinventing ourselves, breaking from Europe as well as our own past, always moving forward. "We are a people," observed Lillian Hellman, "who do not want to keep much of the past in our heads. It is considered unhealthy in America to remember mistakes, neurotic to think about them, psychotic to dwell upon them."[25]

Actually, however, the past stays with us: sometimes it is "not even past."[26] We find ourselves looking again at what happened and also imagining what might have been. "Looking" suggests the metaphor of history as a mirror — one that can enable us to see ourselves.[27] History can also help us reach toward what art and literature seek — to create something that, as Paul Klee explained, "does not reproduce what we see" but rather "makes us see." This very act of reflection can sometimes cause us to regret. However, this emotion is both necessary and human.[28]

But Truman repeatedly stated that he refused to regret. "Never, never waste a minute on regret," he sermonized. "It is a waste of time."[29] Throughout his presidency, Truman presented himself as a man of great self-assurance. Behind Truman's exterior of confidence and conviction, however, was an intricate personality, driven by an inferiority complex, notions of race, a need to be resolute and masculine, and feelings of ambivalence, as well as remorse. His letters to his wife, Bess, private conversations, and Potsdam diary reveal that he was a thoughtful man who dreaded using the atomic bomb and did, subsequently, experience regret over it.

Truman demands attention in our study. As a reporter recalled about the crucial year of 1945, Truman "was *there,* not in the eye of the storm, he *was* the eye of the storm. He did it, all of it."[30] Truman is the key to understanding why America dropped the atomic bomb on Hiroshima.

Our very reaching for understanding has encountered bewildering opposition and acrimony. "What is needed," the *New York Times* noted in a 1994 editorial on the controversy over the Smithsonian's *Enola Gay* exhibit, "is a balanced accounting of the political and military considerations that went into President Truman's decision. There has been an unresolved half-century debate about the morality of that decision."[31]

Indeed, as we revisit Hiroshima historically, we need to have a serious and substantive debate, not casual and uninformed opinions or angry attacks on the Smithsonian that suppress many facts and stifle discussion. Imposing only one version of history based on a narrow and biased selection of evidence — what can be termed "political correctness" — is wrong, whether it comes from the left or the right. What is needed is historical accuracy.

For this debate, institutions of culture and knowledge have the responsibility to make facts available to the American public. They can also serve as forums for discussions, even disagreements, conducted with civility. All of us owe it to ourselves to examine critically as many of the facts as possible and consider differing viewpoints. Moreover, we are entitled to have this debate, as Americans committed to our constitutional right of free speech — one of the "four freedoms" for which Americans bravely fought and died during World War II.

2

"SEVERAL SUNS IN MIDDAY"

> I was born and reared in Hartford, in the State of
> Connecticut. . . . So I am a Yankee of Yankees —
> and practical; yes, and nearly barren of sentiment,
> I suppose — or poetry, in other words. My father
> was a blacksmith, my uncle a horse doctor, and I
> was both, along at first. Then I went over to the
> great arms factory and learned my real trade;
> learned all there was to it; learned to make every-
> thing; guns, revolvers, cannon, boilers, engines, all
> sorts of labor-saving machinery. Why, I could make
> anything. . . .
>
> HANK MORGAN
>
> Mark Twain, *A Connecticut Yankee
> in King Arthur's Court*[1]

The Creation of a New "Colossal Reality"[2]

In the late afternoon of April 12, 1945, Vice President Harry
Truman strolled into the private office of Sam Rayburn. He had
been invited by the Speaker of the House, a bachelor from
Texas, to join a small gathering of men for some "libation."[3]

As Truman mixed himself a drink of bourbon and water, he
was told to phone press secretary Steve Early at the White
House immediately. "Please come over here as quickly and qui-
etly as you can," said Early.[4] Truman was not told why he was
wanted at the White House; still, he instantly sensed that some-

thing of immense significance was occurring. "Jesus Christ and General Jackson," he exclaimed as he returned the receiver.[5] "Boys," he told everyone, "this is in the room. Keep this quiet. Something must have happened."[6] Abruptly leaving his drink and his colleagues, he raced to the White House.

In the sitting room of the private quarters, Eleanor Roosevelt announced: "Harry, the President is dead."[7]

The news "stunned" Truman.[8] But he quickly composed himself and offered his help to Mrs. Roosevelt. Perspicaciously, the First Lady replied: "Is there anything we can do for you? For you are the one in trouble now."[9]

Suddenly, Truman had become president. Alone, a few hours later, he felt such "great emotion" that he "shed tears," thinking about "the responsibility," "the awful responsibility."[10]

Earlier that evening, Truman, as the new president, had been given a glimpse into something "almost unbelievable." He held a brief cabinet meeting; after adjournment, he noticed that the secretary of war had lingered. Henry Stimson had stayed behind to tell Truman that the United States was building "the most destructive weapon in history." Truman recalled that this "first bit of information" about the atomic bomb had left him feeling "puzzled."[11]

Actually, Truman had suspected that something "unusually important" was being developed in the war plants. As a senator, he had been chairman of the Committee to Investigate the National Defense Program, and had tried to find out why so much money was being spent for "certain enormous constructions" in Washington and Tennessee. When Secretary of War Stimson learned about Truman's probe, he phoned the senator and requested a private meeting.

"Senator," Stimson said, "I can't tell you what it is, but it is the greatest project in the history of the world. It is most top secret. Many of the people who are actually engaged in the work have no idea what it is, and we who do would appreciate your not going into these plants."

Truman respected Stimson as a patriot and statesman. "I'll take you at your word," he replied. "I'll order the investigations into those plants called off."[12] The senator added: "You don't need to tell me anything else."[13]

Now, as the new president, Truman had to be told everything, and he was briefed by Stimson about the research project on the atomic bomb. The next day, former director of war mobilization James Byrnes gave Truman some details about how the United States was perfecting an explosive "great enough to destroy the whole world." "Almost incredible developments" were underway, Truman realized, and an "awful power" might "soon" be placed in his hands.[14]

Two weeks later, Truman found out how soon that would be. On April 25, Stimson informed Truman: "Within four months we shall in all probability have completed the most terrible weapon ever known in human history, one bomb of which could destroy a whole city."[15]

That power became a reality on July 16, at an Indian reservation in New Mexico called Alamogordo. "For the first time in history there was a nuclear explosion," Stimson read from a report to Truman. "And what an explosion!" The blast illuminated the sky. "For a brief period there was a lighting effect within a radius of 20 miles equal to several suns in midday; a huge ball of fire was formed which lasted for several seconds." In a blaze of colors, "golden, purple, violet, gray and blue," lighting "every peak, crevasse and ridge of the nearby mountain range," the exploding ball "mushroomed" and "rose to a height of over ten thousand feet."[16]

Brigadier General Thomas F. Farrell witnessed the blast from a control shelter only ten thousand yards away and heard an "awesome roar which warned of doomsday."[17] Atomic scientist

Philip Morrison was ten miles away: "We saw the unbelievably brilliant flash. That was not the most impressive thing. We knew it was going to be blinding. We wore welder's glasses. The thing that got me was not the flash but the blinding heat of a bright day on your face in the cold desert morning. It was like opening a hot oven with the sun coming out like a sunrise."[18]

At Base Camp, Isidor Rabi saw something horrifying, almost alive. "Suddenly, there was an enormous flash of light, the brightest light I have ever seen." The creature seemed animated: "It blasted; it pounced; it bored its way right through you." Rabi felt a piercing fear: "There was an enormous ball of fire which grew and grew and it rolled as it grew; it went up into the air, in yellow flashes and into scarlet and green. It looked menacing. It seemed to come toward one."[19]

After the blast had passed, Los Alamos Laboratory director J. Robert Oppenheimer left the shelter and entered a universe transformed. "We knew the world would not be the same," he reported. "A few people laughed, a few people cried." Most of them were silent, however. As Oppenheimer tried to comprehend what had just occurred, he remembered a line from the Hindu scripture the *Bhagavad Gita*. In order to persuade the Prince to do his duty, Vishnu assumed his many-armed form and warned: "Now I am become Death, the shatterer of worlds."[20]

At Potsdam, a few days later, the new destructive force stirred Truman to reflect in his diary: "We have discovered the most terrible bomb in the history of the world. It may be the fire destruction prophesied in the Euphrates Valley Era, after Noah and his fabulous Ark. . . ." Details of the blast fascinated Truman. "Thirteen pounds of the explosive," he recorded in his diary, "caused the complete disintegration of a steel tower 60 feet high, created a crater 6 feet deep and 1,200 feet in diameter, knocked over a steel tower 1/2 mile away and knocked men down 10,000 yards away. The explosion was visible for more than 200 miles and audible for 40 miles and more."[21] Like Mark Twain's Connecticut Yankee, Americans had again proven that they could make "anything."[22]

The Manhattan Project: Whither the Bomb?

At this point, the war in Europe had ended, and the question was whether this new weapon would be used against Japan. The U.S. had initially begun research on the atomic bomb because of a fear that the Nazis were developing nuclear weapons.

Even before the outbreak of the war, scientists had known that it was theoretically possible to create an atomic bomb. One of them was Leo Szilard. In 1933, the Hungarian scientist was in London, where he had fled when Hitler came to power in Germany. Szilard had been standing at an intersection, waiting for a red light to change, and was thinking about the theoretical complexity of transforming atoms, and about chain reactions. "As the light changed to green and I crossed the street," he recalled, "it . . . suddenly occurred to me that if we could find an element which is split by neutrons and which would emit *two* neutrons when it absorbs *one* neutron, such an element, if assembled in sufficiently large mass, could sustain a nuclear reaction." At that moment, Szilard did not know how to find such an element or how to split an atom. But he realized that "in certain circumstances it might be possible to set up a nuclear chain reaction, liberate energy on an industrial scale, and construct atomic bombs."[23]

Six years later, Szilard, working in the United States, became apprehensive about the threat of German atomic research and decided to warn Roosevelt. He approached Albert Einstein and asked him to write a letter to the president. The famous scientist agreed and dictated a short draft in German, which Szilard reworked.[24]

In this letter, dated August 2, 1939, Einstein urged President Roosevelt to pursue research on the atomic bomb. "It may become possible," the eminent scientist explained, "to set up a nuclear chain reaction in a large mass of uranium, by which vast amounts of power and large quantities of new radium-like elements would be generated." This breakthrough, Einstein continued, could lead to the development of a bomb capable of destroying a whole port and its surrounding territory. Ominously, Einstein noted: "I understand Germany has actually stopped the sale of uranium from Czechoslovakian mines which she has taken over."[25]

The letter was delivered to Roosevelt by Dr. Alexander Sachs, a director of Lehman Brothers Investment Corporation. The message provoked worry. "Alex," the President said, "what you are after is to see that the Nazis don't blow us up." Roosevelt gave the letter to his personal secretary, Edwin M. "Pa" Watson, and instructed: "Pa, this requires action."[26] Thus was launched a two-billion-dollar atomic-weapons program known as the Manhattan Project — what Twain would certainly have called a "great arms factory" magnified a million times.[27]

The intended target of the bomb was Germany. In a report dated December 16, 1942, Vannevar Bush, chairman of the Office of Scientific Research and Development, informed Roosevelt: "There can no longer be any question that atomic energy may be released under controlled conditions and used as power." Furthermore, Bush emphasized, this same energy could be employed to create "a super-explosive of overwhelming military might." He then compared America's project with German atomic research. "We still do not know where we stand in the race with the enemy toward a usable result, but it is quite possible that Germany is ahead of us and may well be able to produce superbombs sooner than we can."[28]

Actually, Germany was not ahead of the United States. According to Albert Speer, minister of armaments and war production, Hitler had spoken to him about the possibility of an atomic bomb, "but the idea quite obviously strained his intellectual capacity." In 1942, told that it would take about three or four years to develop an atomic bomb, Speer decided to "scuttle" the project. After the war, German scientist Werner Heisenberg stated that he and his fellow physicists were "spared the decision as to whether or not they should aim at producing atomic bombs."[29]

Stimson and Bush had doubts about German progress on the bomb. In his diary on June 10, 1944, the secretary of war noted that the successful American bombing of the German atomic research installation had "probably" put them back and that the German scientists were "not ahead of us." On December 13, Stimson recorded in his diary that Bush believed the German scientists were in "the latter stages of the experimental process but [had] not yet embarked on the highly expensive production."[30]

Still, many American policymakers and scientists continued to view Germany as a very dangerous nuclear threat. "From January, 1939, until American troops finally entered Germany and we took into custody a number of the senior German scientists," Manhattan Project director General Leslie Groves wrote, "we faced the definite possibility that Germany would produce a nuclear weapon before we could."[31] Atomic scientist Arthur H. Compton described their anxiety: "So acute was our concern about Germany's progress that when the Allies landed on the Normandy beaches on 6 June 1944, certain of the American officers were equipped with Geiger counters."[32] President Roosevelt had been prepared to use the atomic bomb against Germany. In 1944, according to General Groves, Roosevelt told him that "if the European war was not over before we had our first bombs he wanted us to be ready to drop them on Germany."[33]

On May 7, however, Germany surrendered. No longer did there seem to be a need to continue research on the atomic bomb. "Initially," atomic scientist Szilard said, "we were motivated to produce the bomb because we feared the Germans would get ahead of us and the only way to prevent them from dropping bombs on us was to have bombs in readiness ourselves. But now, with the war won, it was not clear what we were working for."[34]

Despite the defeat of Germany, however, the Manhattan Project continued and, in fact, intensified. "I don't think there was any time when we worked harder at the speedup than in the period after the German surrender," recalled Los Alamos director J. Robert Oppenheimer.[35]

The reason for this acceleration was not the possibility of a Japanese atomic threat. Japan lacked the resources and technical knowledge to become a nuclear power. According to historian John Dower, the facts on this issue clearly show that Japan did engage in atomic research, but that its accomplishments were "minuscule and miserable" and indicated the relative backwardness of Japanese science and technology.[36] Manhattan Project director General Groves was not at all concerned about Japan as a potential atomic competitor. "Japan did not in our opinion," he wrote, "have the industrial capacity, the scientific manpower or the essential raw material." He elaborated that "there was not even the remotest possibility that Japan had enough uranium or uranium ore to produce the necessary materials for a nuclear weapon."[37] American research on the bomb, initially intended for defense, had now acquired a purpose different from its original one.

"I can't tell you what this [the atomic project] is, Grace [Tully]," Roosevelt reportedly told his secretary, "but if it works, and pray God that it does, it will save many American lives."[38] Roosevelt was thinking of the casualties that would be incurred in an invasion of Japan. At the Hyde Park meeting of September 19, 1944, Roosevelt and Winston Churchill had agreed that the atomic bomb "might perhaps, after mature consideration, be used against the Japanese."[39] Thus, Roosevelt did not think that the new weapon would necessarily be used.

Shortly after signing an aide-mémoire reflecting their verbal agreement, Roosevelt asked Bush whether he thought the atomic bomb "should actually be used against the Japanese or whether it should be used only as a threat with full-scale experimentation in this country."[40] Three months later, on December 30, Stimson showed Roosevelt a report on the schedule for the production of the atomic bombs: a plutonium bomb would be tested in July, and a uranium bomb, which did not require testing, would be ready for combat by August 1.[41]

However, Roosevelt had not actually made a firm decision to use the atomic bomb in combat against Japan. In a top secret memorandum dated September 30, 1944, Bush and J. B. Conant, chairman of the National Defense Research Committee, had recommended that plans be made for the "complete disclosure" of the bomb's development and all but its manufacturing and military details as soon as "the first bomb had been demonstrated." This "demonstration" might be over "enemy territory" or in "our own country." Afterward, Japan would be warned that the new weapon would be used against Japan unless surrender was forthcoming.[42]

Then, in December, Roosevelt told Alexander Sachs that the

bomb would be used against both Germany and Japan if necessary. But first the weapon would be demonstrated, and an ultimatum issued.[43] That was Roosevelt's last known word on the bomb before his death. Whether or not to deploy the bomb in combat still seemed tentative.

Seven months later, Truman authorized the bombing of Japanese cities. Why did he make this decision?

3

TO SAVE "HALF A MILLION" AMERICAN LIVES

Some of us consider the bomb in the same category as poison gas and were against its use on a civilian population. Others were of the opinion that in total war, as carried on in Japan, there was no difference between civilians and soldiers, and that the bomb itself was an effective force tending to end the bloodshed, warning Japan to surrender and thus to avoid total destruction. It seems logical that he who supports total war in principle cannot complain of a war against civilians. The crux of the matter is whether total war in its present form is justifiable, even when it serves a just purpose. Does it not have material and spiritual evil as its consequences which far exceed whatever good might result? When will our moralists give us a clear answer to this question?

Father Siemes, German Jesuit priest in Japan, shortly after the bomb[1]

The Report to the Joint Chiefs of Staff

Truman took responsibility for unleashing the atomic bomb against Japan. As president and commander in chief of the United States Armed Forces, he possessed the authority. Truman explained the reason for his decision: to avoid an invasion of Japan and thus save "half a million" American lives.[2]

The atomic bomb did render an invasion unnecessary, and it did hasten the end of the war. However, as Truman himself knew, what happened was much more complicated.

Where did Truman get his figure for battle deaths? "General Marshall told me," the retired president wrote, "that it might cost half a million American lives to force the enemy's surrender on his home grounds."[3] This statement was made in Truman's memoirs, published in 1955, ten years after the bombing of Hiroshima. Unfortunately, since his memoirs do not have footnotes, one cannot check the source of Truman's information.

Both Truman and General George Marshall knew, however, that the actual casualty estimates for an invasion of Japan were significantly lower. In fact, in June of 1945, Truman had ordered the military to calculate the cost in American lives for the planned assault on Japan. He stated that he wanted to "know how far we could afford to go in the Japanese campaign." Aware of the bloody fighting that had already occurred in the Pacific, Truman hoped to prevent "an Okinawa from one end of Japan to the other." American losses in Okinawa had been extremely heavy: 41,700, including killed, wounded, and missing.[4]

In response to Truman's request for estimates, the Joint War Plans Committee prepared a report for the Chiefs of Staff, dated June 15, 1945. They gave the following estimates of casualties:[5]

	Killed	Wounded	Missing	Total
Southern Kyushu, followed by Tokyo Plain	40,000	150,000	3500	193,500

The plan was first to invade Japan's southern island of Kyushu on November 1, followed by an invasion of the Tokyo Plain, on the main island of Honshu, in March. The estimate for the total number that would be killed was not 500,000, but 40,000.

On June 18, General Douglas MacArthur concurred with the Joint War Plans Committee's low estimates. In a memo, "Urgent from General MacArthur to General Marshall," which was attached to the report, the supreme commander of the Allied forces in the Pacific stated that he did not anticipate a "high rate of loss" of life and casualties in an attack on Japan. "I regard the operation as the most economical one in effort and lives that is possible."[6]

The Joint War Plans Committee thought that the invasion of Japan would be different from the assault on Okinawa, and, hence, that losses would be lighter. For one thing, the Tokyo Plain had many more beaches "suitable for amphibious assault"; this geography would "preclude [the] concentration of defense." Furthermore, the terrain of the Tokyo Plain would permit American forces to exploit their "superiority in maneuver and equipment." Therefore, the military planners concluded, "in terms of percentage of casualties the invasion of the Tokyo Plain should be relatively inexpensive."[7]

On June 18, Truman met with the Joint Chiefs of Staff at the White House. General Marshall was present, and the minutes of the meeting indicate that he participated in the discussions. Truman undoubtedly had prepared for the meeting by reading the June 15 report of the Joint War Plans Committee. He was an extremely conscientious reader of reports. According to Assistant Secretary of State Dean Acheson, "Mr. Truman read the documents themselves, and he understood and acted on them."[8]

During the discussion on casualties at the meeting with the Joint Chiefs of Staff, Truman was assured that the invasion of Japan would not be another Okinawa. In fact, he was told that there was "reason to believe that the first 30 days in Kyushu should not exceed the price we have paid for Luzon [31,000 casualties, killed, wounded, missing]." The Kyushu assault, the military chiefs confirmed, would be different from the deadly battle for the conquest of Okinawa. "There had been only one way to go on Okinawa," explained Admiral Ernest King. "This meant a straight frontal attack against a highly fortified position. On Kyushu, however, landings would be made on three fronts simultaneously and there would be much more room for maneuver." Thus, in King's view, a "realistic" casualty figure for Kyushu would lie "somewhere between" the number experienced in the operations in Luzon and Okinawa.[9]

Clearly, the military planners had informed Truman directly that they expected American casualties to be "relatively inexpensive." According to the minutes of the meeting, Truman said he understood that "the Joint Chiefs of Staff, after weighing all the possibilities of the situation and considering all possible alternative plans, were still of the unanimous opinion that the Kyushu operation was the best solution under the circumstances." Then he told the Joint Chiefs of Staff that the Kyushu plan was "all right from a military standpoint" and ordered them to "go ahead with it."[10]

The atomic bomb was not mentioned in these deliberations on the invasion. "We still hadn't decided," Truman recalled after he retired, "whether or not to use the atomic bomb."[11] In his diary, on June 17, he asked himself: "I have to decide Japanese strategy — shall we invade Japan proper or shall we bomb and blockade? That is my hardest decision to date. But I'll make it when I have all the facts."[12]

Before Hiroshima: The Path toward Total War

In June, Truman still had not made up his mind about dropping the bomb, but by then the nature of warfare was being redefined. Developments in the air war in Europe and Japan were opening the way toward total war and, ultimately, the dropping of the atomic bomb.

"For nearly two hundred years," wrote historian Ronald Schaffer, "a model of war had developed in the West which held that, if at all possible, inhabitants of 'civilized' nations should be spared from attack, great cities preserved, and the artifacts of high culture left unharmed." Exceptions occurred, but the model itself had remained intact through World War I.[13]

During that conflict, President Woodrow Wilson had defined what was moral and permissible in warfare: "I desire no sort of participation by the Air Service of the United States in a plan . . . which has as its object promiscuous bombing upon industry, commerce, or populations in enemy countries disassociated from obvious military needs to be served by such action." According to Schaffer, this view remained official War Department policy through World War II, "at least on paper."[14]

During World War II, President Roosevelt had denounced as immoral the Japanese air attack on Chungking and also the 1939 Russian bombing of Helsinki: "The American Government and the American people have for some time pursued a policy of wholeheartedly condemning the unprovoked bombing and machine-gunning of civilian populations from the air."[15]

As the war continued, however, technological advances and the increasing use of air power began to undermine the ethical view that civilians should not be targeted. What occurred, according to Schaffer, was "a revolution in the morality of warfare." After German planes started bombing London, the British Royal Air Force retaliated with raids designed to disrupt the German economy by "dehousing," killing, and terrorizing workers. Based in England, the U.S. Army Air Force initially refused to join the British in these destructive air attacks. General Hap Arnold explained in 1943: "We want the people to understand and have faith in *our way of making war*."[16] He did not want to violate the widely held American moral view that the war should be fought against soldiers, not civilians.

But the air war in Europe continued to expand, and American air forces were swept into the new tactic of mass bombing. Even General Arnold's thinking changed. War was "horrible," he admitted, and the bomber simply added to the extent of the horror, "especially if not used with discretion." However, he rationalized: "When used with the proper degree of understanding," bombing could become "in effect, the most humane of all weapons." In April 1943, Arnold told his air staff: "This is a brutal war and . . . the way to stop the killing of civilians is to cause so much damage and destruction and death that the civilians will demand their government cease fighting."[17] Hence, mass destruction by air power could help end the war.

This air strategy reached new heights of violence with the assault on Dresden. On February 13–14, 1945, the city was burned and literally leveled. Estimates of the number killed varied from 35,000 to as many as 135,000. The destruction unnerved John Kenneth Galbraith, who was serving as a member of an independent civilian commission to review the way the air force was conducting the war. "All of war is cruel and unnecessary," he recalled years later, "but the bombings made this one especially so. The destruction of Dresden was unforgivable." Henry Hatfield, who worked in the Office of War Information, commented: "[The bombing of] Dresden is the one thing I'm really ashamed of. I mean hellishly sorry. It was an open city, full of refugees coming back from the eastern front. Who can say that wrecking this beautiful, nonmilitary city shortened the war?"[18]

Meanwhile, this pattern of wholesale destruction was also occurring in Japan. On March 9–10, the firebombing of Tokyo killed 83,000 people, most of them civilians. During the raid, General Thomas Power flew over the burning city. "I watched block after block go up in flames," he reported, "until the holocaust had spread into a seething, swirling ocean of fire, engulfing the city below for miles in every direction." The scene below horrified Power. "True there is no room for emotions in war," he admitted. "But the destruction I witnessed that night over Tokyo was so overwhelming that it left a tremendous and lasting impression on me."[19] Brigadier General Bonner Fellers described the American air raids as "one of the most ruthless and barbaric killings of non-combatants in all history."[20] The distinction between military and civilian casualties had now been blurred, as air power carried destruction directly to cities.

Justifying this bombing of Tokyo, General Curtis LeMay pointed out that civilians were living near arms factories and that war-related industries were dispersed throughout the city. "Even little kids" were helping at home to manufacture weapons, "working all day." LeMay viewed the expansion of the air war as a military necessity: "No matter how you slice it, you're going to kill an awful lot of civilians. Thousands and thousands. But, if you don't destroy the Japanese industry, we're going to have to invade Japan. And how many Americans will be killed in an invasion of Japan? Five hundred thousand seems to be the lowest estimate. . . . We're at war with Japan. We were attacked by Japan. Do you want to kill Japanese, or would you rather have Americans killed?"[21]

A spokesman for the Fifth Air Force argued that since the Japanese government was mobilizing civilians to resist invasion, "the entire population of Japan is a proper military target."[22] Colonel Harry F. Cunningham put it bluntly: "We military men do not pull punches or put on Sunday School picnics. We are making War and making it in the all-out fashion which saves American lives, shortens the agony which War is and seeks to bring about an enduring Peace. We intend to seek out and destroy the enemy wherever he or she is, in the greatest possible numbers, in the shortest possible time. For us, THERE ARE NO CIVILIANS IN JAPAN."[23] This kind of thinking generated a certain military logic that would rapidly and inexorably lead to the use of the atomic bomb.

In January, 1943, *Harper's* justified the firebombing of Japanese cities as a means to shorten the war and avoid an invasion. "It seems brutal to be talking about burning homes," the magazine argued. "But we are engaged in a life and death struggle for national survival, and we are therefore justified in taking any action which will save the lives of American soldiers and sailors. We must strike hard with everything we have."[24]

After the destruction of Hiroshima, the *New Republic* responded to the criticism that the atomic bomb had murdered thousands of noncombatants, including women and children. The "same objection," the editor argued, applied with "equal force to the strategic bombing of enemy cities."[25] In other words, the infliction of massive civilian deaths on occasions prior to Hiroshima was the rationale for doing it again.

This was the way the atomic bombing was viewed by a soldier who had been scheduled to participate in the invasion of Japan: "Our B-29's for months were flying over Tokyo and Yokohama, dropping firebombs. We were deliberately trying to burn everybody to death in those two cities. So what was worse?"[26]

The expansion of the air war led to Dresden and Hiroshima: both cities were obliterated. But, contrary to Kurt Vonnegut's simplistic comparison in his novel *Slaughterhouse-Five,* the two bombings were not alike in origins or intent. The demolition of Dresden represented revenge for German air attacks on civilians in London and Coventry. Though Japan had not engaged in the massive and indiscriminate bombing of American cities, it also became the target of wholesale destruction. Why and how did this happen?

Eisenhower: "Grave Misgivings"

The use of the atomic bomb did end the Pacific war, but whether it was militarily necessary was questioned at the time by several of America's most important military leaders.

By July of 1945, Japan's military situation was extremely precarious. The Joint War Plans Committee was confident of victory. In its June 15 report, it described the disarray of the Japanese defense: "Already we have eliminated practically all Japanese sea traffic between their main islands and points to the southward of Shanghai."[27] Japan's main army was in China, cut off from supplies and reinforcements, targeted for total destruction by Chinese and Russian forces then mobilizing.

At Potsdam, General Dwight D. Eisenhower, supreme commander of Allied forces in Western Europe, told Stimson that the atomic bomb should not be used. Voicing his "grave misgivings," he explained that Japan was "already defeated": Japan was "at that very moment" seeking some way to surrender with "a minimum loss of face." Dropping the bomb, the general argued, would be "completely unnecessary." Furthermore, the United States should "avoid shocking world opinion by the use of a weapon whose employment was . . . no longer mandatory as a measure to save American lives." Eisenhower also hoped the U.S. would not be the first to deploy a weapon so "horrible." The general recalled that as he discussed the bomb with Stimson, he had become "conscious of a feeling of depression."[28]

General Douglas MacArthur, supreme commander of Allied forces in the Pacific, was not even consulted about the use of the bomb. When he found out about the decision for the atomic attack, he thought it was "completely unnecessary from a military point of view."[29] Notice of the decision was given to MacArthur only two days before the scheduled attack.[30] "General MacArthur didn't know [about the order to drop the bomb on Hiroshima]," army chief of staff George Marshall told a reporter, "until just before the bombs were sent out to the Pacific."[31]

Late on the afternoon of August 6, MacArthur called a press conference. He told the reporters that his remarks would be "off the record," but James H. Halsema of the *Manila Daily Bulletin* took some notes. According to Halsema, MacArthur said that the war might "end sooner than some think." The Japanese were "already beaten." MacArthur pointed out that their navy was impotent and their shipping had been destroyed. The general concluded by saying that he was already thinking about the peace, as well as "the possibilities of a next war with its horrors magnified 10,000 times." Very shortly after this meeting, the electrifying news of the bombing of Hiroshima reached Manila.[32]

Both Eisenhower and MacArthur thought Japan's defeat was imminent. Chief of staff Admiral William D. Leahy insisted that even an invasion of Japan was unnecessary to end the war: "I was unable to see any justification, from a national-defense point of view, for an invasion of an already thoroughly defeated Japan." Leahy calculated that it would be too costly in American lives to invade Japan in order to extract an unconditional surrender. The navy alone, he thought, could bring an end to the war. "My conclusion, with which the naval representatives agreed, was that America's least expensive course of action was to continue to intensify the air and sea blockade and at the same time occupy the Philippines. I believed that a completely blockaded Japan would then fall by its own weight."[33]

Convinced Japan was on the verge of collapse, Admiral Leahy was willing to accept a conditional surrender and proclaim victory.[34] In his private diary on June 18, 1945, the chief of staff recorded: "It is my opinion at the present time that a surrender of Japan can be arranged with terms that can be accepted by Japan and that will make fully satisfactory provision for America's defense against future trans-Pacific aggression."[35] Leahy also pointed out that a conditional surrender that would allow the Japanese people to keep their emperor seemed to be consistent with the Atlantic Charter's promise that Great Britain and the United States would "respect the right of all peoples to choose the form of government under which they will live."[36]

Thus, three very important and highly respected military leaders — Eisenhower, MacArthur, and Leahy — did not think the atomic bombing of Hiroshima was a military necessity. Their views were confirmed shortly after the war. In a 1946 report, the U.S. Bombing Survey concluded that "certainly prior to 31 December 1945 and in all probability prior to 1 November 1945 [the date of the planned Kyushu invasion], Japan would have surrendered even if the bombs had not been dropped, even if Russia had not entered the war, and even if no invasion had been planned or contemplated."[37]

According to military planners, the war was virtually over even within Japan itself. The cities had been reduced to rubble, activities of work and life had been severely disrupted, and the people themselves were dispirited. On June 29, the Joint Chiefs of Staff discussed plans for the occupation of Japan. One of the items on the meeting's agenda stated: "Prepare for sudden collapse of Japan."[38] A week later, a top secret report prepared for the Combined Chiefs of Staff meetings at Potsdam gave an "Estimate of the Enemy Situation":

> We believe that a considerable portion of the Japanese population now consider absolute military defeat to be probable. The increasing effects of sea blockade and cumulative devastation wrought by strategic bombing, which has already rendered millions homeless and has destroyed from 25% to 50% of the built-up area

of Japan's most important cities, should make this realization increasingly general. An entry of the Soviet Union into the war would finally convince the Japanese of the inevitability of complete defeat. Although individual Japanese willingly sacrifice themselves in the service of the nation, we doubt that the nation as a whole is predisposed toward national suicide.

The report also noted that "a conditional surrender by the Japanese Government . . . might be offered by them at any time from now until the time of the complete destruction of all Japanese power of resistance."[39]

Indeed, at that very moment, Japan was seeking a way to negotiate a conditional surrender. After the country's terrible and decisive defeat in Okinawa in June, Emperor Hirohito and his chief political adviser, Marquis Koichi Kido, were anxious to bring the war to an end. In early April, peace policy advocates had gained two crucial positions in the government — Admiral Kantaro Suzuki became premier, and Shigemori Togo, the foreign minister.[40] This new leadership asked Moscow to help negotiate a peace. But only a conditional peace would be acceptable. On July 21, the Japanese government instructed its representative in Moscow: "We cannot consent to unconditional surrender under any circumstances. Even if the war drags on and more blood must be shed, so long as the enemy demands unconditional surrender, we will fight as one man against the enemy in accordance with the Emperor's command."[41]

U.S. intelligence had intercepted these Japanese diplomatic messages asking Russia to facilitate a negotiation for peace. At Potsdam, Stalin read Truman a communication from the Japanese ambassador to Moscow requesting that the Soviet government mediate the end of the conflict.[42] Japan's only concern was whether or not surrender would require the abolition of the emperor system.

The Origins of the Term "Unconditional Surrender"

The United States had already stipulated, however, that the surrender had to be "unconditional." The origins of the term, historian Leon V. Sigal wrote, suggest that "it was intended more as propaganda than as a war aim."[43] At the Casablanca conference of January 1943, Winston Churchill said that the United States and Great Britain might consider issuing a declaration that they would fight "relentlessly" until both Germany and Japan offered an "unconditional surrender." Churchill thought the declaration would "stimulate" U.S. and British "friends in every country"[44] and help energize the war effort. Roosevelt also understood the rallying effect of such a defining statement. In his annual message to Congress, given a month after the Japanese attack on Pearl Harbor, Roosevelt had declared: "There never has been — there never can be — successful compromise between good and evil. Only total victory can reward the champions of tolerance, and decency, and faith."[45]

In the end, the joint communiqué from Casablanca did not mention the term "unconditional surrender." But this phrase became pivotal in the entire drama leading to the bombing of Hiroshima. The way it happened seems to have been largely unplanned. In a press conference after the Casablanca meeting, Roosevelt told a story to the reporters: "Some of you Britishers know the old story — we had a general called U. S. Grant. His name was Ulysses Simpson Grant, but in my, and the Prime Minister's, early days he was called 'Unconditional Surrender' Grant. The elimination of German, Japanese, and Italian war power means [their] unconditional surrender. . . ."[46] Roosevelt's use of the term surprised Churchill.[47] The word "unconditional," historian Richard Rhodes noted, was inserted "ad lib."[48] Thus the term was introduced unofficially, and perhaps inadvertently.

At another press conference a week later, in Washington, Roosevelt repeated what he had said at Casablanca: "We formally reemphasized what we had been talking about before, and that is we don't think there should be any kind of negotiated armistice, for obvious reasons. There ought to be an unconditional surrender."[49] In July 1944, Roosevelt returned to the term implicitly: "Practically all Germans deny the fact they surrendered in the last war, but this time they are going to know it. And so are the Japs."[50]

As the new president, Truman followed Roosevelt's lead in this matter. By then, unconditional surrender had become a popular war aim. On May 8, the end of the European war, Truman told the American people that the military effort would now turn full force to the Pacific war. "The Japanese people have felt the weight of our land, air and naval attacks. So long as their leaders and the armed forces continue the war, the striking power and intensity of our blows will steadily increase, and will bring utter destruction to Japan's industrial war production, to its shipping, and to everything that supports its military activity. . . . Our blows will not cease until the Japanese military and naval forces lay down their arms in *unconditional surrender*."[51]

What Truman inherited from Roosevelt was a war slogan, not a policy. Churchill had been present at Casablanca and understood the original propaganda purpose of the rhetorical term; therefore, he thought that the Allies should not enforce it rigidly. In his discussion with Truman at Potsdam, Churchill questioned whether it made sense to coerce Japan into unconditional surrender. Fighting to the end, Churchill said, would inflict a "tremendous cost in American and to a smaller extent in British life." The surrender terms might be "expressed in some other way," so that the Allies would be able to secure all of "the essentials for future peace and security" and yet leave the Japanese with "some show of saving their military honor and some assurance of their national existence." Truman adamantly rejected this proposal. Churchill, however, persisted. The Japanese had "something for which they were ready to face certain death in very large numbers," he maintained, "and this might not be so important to us as it is to them."[52]

Several of Truman's policymakers also wished to consider offering Japan a conditional surrender. On May 28, Acting Secretary of State Joseph Grew advised Truman to issue a proclamation urging the Japanese to surrender but assuring them that the U.S. would permit the emperor to remain as head of state. A career diplomat, Grew had served as ambassador to Japan from 1932 to 1941 and understood Japanese history and culture. "The greatest obstacle to unconditional surrender by the Japanese," Grew told Truman, "is their belief that this would entail the destruction or permanent removal of the Emperor and the institution of the Throne." The U.S. should let the Japanese "save face" and should give some indication that they would be allowed to determine their own political structure after the war.[53] Truman seemed to agree with this suggestion. "Grew backed this with arguments taken from ten years' experience as our Ambassador to Japan," Truman noted in his memoir, "and I told him that I had already given thought to this matter myself and that it seemed to me a sound idea."[54]

At a meeting of the Joint Chiefs of Staff a month later, Grew told Truman that the proposal for a conditional surrender had been approved by his cabinet colleagues and the Joint Chiefs.[55] In the discussion, Admiral William Leahy expressed his fear that "our insistence on unconditional surrender would result only in making the Japanese desperate and thereby increase our casualty lists." He added that this was not "at all necessary." The president replied that "it was with that thought in mind" that he had "left the door open" for Congress to take appropriate action regarding unconditional surrender. However, Truman added that he did not feel he could "take any action at this time to change public opinion on the matter."[56]

A Gallup poll in July showed that one-third of the people surveyed wanted to execute Emperor Hirohito as a war criminal, and twenty percent wanted to have him jailed or exiled. Only seven percent wanted to allow him to remain as emperor.[57] But views on the emperor question were diverse. The widely read *Life* magazine, for example, urged the United States to allow the emperor to remain. The editors defined what they considered acceptable terms for ending the war: Japan's forfeiture of its colonies and the territories it had seized, dismantlement of its war industry, surrender of its military, and punishment of war criminals. "There would be a short-term occupation of Japan, but eventually we would withdraw, leaving the Japanese to govern themselves. The Potsdam ultimatum is silent on the subject of the Emperor, but a penitent Japan might even be allowed to keep what our State Department calls the 'imperial institution.'"[58]

At Potsdam, Truman and his policymakers discussed whether the conference's declaration should include an assurance that the Japanese could keep their emperor. There was a division of opinions. In his diary on July 24, Stimson recorded: "I then spoke of the importance which I attributed to the reassurance of the Japanese on the continuance of their dynasty, and I had felt that the insertion of that in the formal warning was important and might be just the thing that would make or mar their acceptance, but that I had heard from [Secretary of State James] Byrnes that they preferred not to put it in. . . ."[59] "They" included the president.

Truman had been pulled into the popular expectation that Japan would have to surrender unconditionally — a legacy from Roosevelt that he was reluctant to revise. After the explosion at Alamogordo, moreover, Truman realized he now had the power to force Japan into total submission. Thus, in the Potsdam Declaration of July 26, Truman issued an ultimatum to Japan to accept "unconditional surrender" or face the "utter devastation of the Japanese homeland."[60]

Without an assurance regarding the emperor, the Potsdam Declaration precluded the possibility of a Japanese surrender. Premier Kantaro Suzuki rejected Truman's final warning by declaring that it was "unworthy of public notice." "In the face of this rejection," Stimson recalled, we could only proceed to demonstrate that the ultimatum meant "exactly what it said."[61]

This Was the Way the War Ended

Long before the Potsdam ultimatum of "unconditional surrender," however, plans and preparations for the deployment of the atomic bomb in combat had been well underway. The immense Manhattan Project was in motion — a bureaucratic industrial colossus, with over 120,000 employees and facilities all over the country, from Hanford, Washington, to Los Alamos, New Mexico, to Chicago, and to Oak Ridge, Tennessee. Atomic scientist Bertrand Goldschmidt described the project as "the astonishing American creation in three years . . . of a formidable array of factories and laboratories — as large as the entire automobile industry of the United States at that date."[62]

The gigantic federal expenditure for this project seemed to require justification — the development of a superbomb for use in the current war. "I understand that the expenditures for the Manhattan Project are approaching two billion dollars with no definite assurance yet of production," Byrnes reported to Roosevelt on March 3, 1945. Byrnes warned of a possible investigation: "We have succeeded to date in obtaining the cooperation of congressional committees in secret hearings. Perhaps we can continue to do so while the war lasts."[63] In the meeting of the

Interim Committee on June 1, General Groves reported that current appropriations for the project would continue through June 1946. Commenting on this information, Byrnes pointed out that "in the event the war ended" before that time, "Congress would be disposed to cancel all outstanding authorizations."[64] So much money had already been committed and spent; what would happen after the war if the project were dismantled or if it failed? In his report to Roosevelt, Byrnes had predicted that there would be "relentless investigation and criticism."[65]

Within this enormously expensive and complex bureaucratic empire, gears within gears had begun to move as early as 1942, slowly at first, and then with increasing velocity. Propelling the Manhattan Project toward Hiroshima was an intricate machinery of committees.

One such gear was the Target Committee, under the authority of Manhattan Project director Groves. On May 11, 1945, this group of military ordnance specialists and Manhattan Project scientists, such as J. Robert Oppenheimer, recommended that the target be a small, strictly military facility, located in a much larger area subject to blast damage. Operating on instructions from General Groves, they proposed that the bomb have "the greatest psychological effect against Japan" and that its "initial use" be "sufficiently spectacular."[66]

The most important gear in the Manhattan machinery was the Interim Committee. Approved by Truman and assembled by Stimson, this group included key atomic scientists like James B. Conant and Oppenheimer, Secretary of War Henry Stimson as chairman, and James Byrnes as the president's personal representative. General George Marshall and General Groves participated as military advisers. This committee had considerable power and responsibility: its charge was to advise the president on the use of the bomb.

During their deliberations on May 31 and June 1, members discussed the suggestion to explode the bomb in a "nonmilitary demonstration" in order to impress Japan's leaders and induce them to surrender. But the idea was rejected. "We could not afford the chance that [the bomb] might be a dud," explained Arthur H. Compton. "If the test were made on some neutral territory, it was hard to believe that Japan's determined and fanatical military men would be impressed. If such an open test were made first and failed to bring surrender, the chance would be gone to give the shock of surprise. . . ."[67]

Instead, the Interim Committee recommended that the atomic bomb be deployed "without prior warning" on a military installation or war industry plant "surrounded by workers' houses." The purpose would be to inflict "a profound psychological impression" on Japan.[68] This choice would certainly demonstrate the bomb's tremendous power. But it also would mean the indiscriminate and mass killing of civilians.

One of the driving influences in the Interim Committee was Byrnes. He had been selected for this committee by Truman and would become secretary of state on July 3. Born in 1882, he was raised by his seamstress mother in South Carolina. Byrnes was nurtured by Southern politicos like Senator Benjamin "Pitchfork Ben" Tillman; he was elected to Congress first as a representative and then as a senator. During the 1930s, he helped steer much of Roosevelt's legislative program through Congress. In 1941, Byrnes was appointed to direct the Office of War Mobilization and became known as the "assistant president." In 1944, he was considered for the vice-presidential nomination. Now Byrnes was again a powerful adviser to the president, this time to Truman.

The minutes of the Interim Committee meetings clearly show that Byrnes was the single most important member promoting the proposal for a surprise atomic attack. The air force had been dropping leaflets on cities to warn civilians to evacuate before a bombing attack. But Byrnes argued against giving a warning. He argued that "if the Japanese were told that the bomb would be used on a given locality, they might bring our boys who were prisoners of war to that area." Also, there was no conclusive proof that the bomb would explode when dropped from an airplane. "If we were to warn the Japanese of the new highly destructive weapon in the hope of impressing them and if the bomb then failed to explode, certainly we would have given aid and comfort to the Japanese militarists."[69]

Like Byrnes, General Groves was also a moving force in the Interim Committee. Born in 1896 in Albany, New York, he graduated from West Point and then served in Hawaii and Nicaragua. Groves was appointed to head the Manhattan Project at its inception: he was the man pulling the gearshifts of the huge atomic-research machinery. He thought the atomic bomb should be used against Japan in order to avoid an invasion and bring the war to a quick end. "Throughout the period when we were planning our atomic bombing operations against Japan," Groves wrote in his memoirs, "American strategy was based upon the assumption that an invasion of the Japanese homeland was essential to ending the war in the Pacific." In his July 18 report on the successful detonation at Alamogordo, Groves wrote: "We are fully conscious that our real goal is still before us. The battle test is what counts in the war with Japan."[70]

The train for the decision to drop the bomb had left the station. At this point, the choice for Truman to make was whether or not to derail existing plans for the "battle test." Although the president had the "primary responsibility" for the decision, Groves explained, "as far as I was concerned, his decision was one of noninterference — basically, a decision not to upset the existing plans."[71] Groves described the President's options: "Truman did not so much say 'yes' as not say 'no.' It would indeed have taken a lot of nerve to say 'no' at that time."[72]

In his diary on July 25, Truman wrote: "This weapon is to be used against Japan between now and August 10. I have told the Sec. of War, Mr. Stimson, to use it so that military objectives and soldiers and sailors are the target and not women and children." The target should be "a purely military one."[73]

But at the same time, Truman also accepted the Interim Committee's recommendation that the bomb be used "against a target that would clearly show its devastating strength." In his memoir, he wrote: "I had realized, of course, that an atomic bomb explosion would inflict damage and casualties beyond imagination."[74] The concern of the Interim Committee and Stimson was that the air strikes against Japanese cities had already left so many of them in rubble and ruin that only a few cities remained intact. Thus, there might be no appropriate target for an atomic attack. According to Stimson's diary, he had told Truman that he was "a little fearful that before we could get ready, the Air Force might have Japan so thoroughly bombed that the new weapon would not have a fair background [against which] to show its strength." Truman "laughed and said he understood."[75]

General Groves gave guidelines for the selection of the target: "To enable us to assess accurately the effects of the bomb, the targets should not have been previously damaged by air raids. It was also desirable that the first target be of such size that the damage would be confined within it, so that we could more definitely determine the power of the bomb."[76] Still untouched by the air war, Hiroshima seemed an ideal target.

On August 6, Japan time [August 5 in the U.S.], the B-29 *Enola Gay* lifted off from the island of Tinian. Colonel William S. Parsons, the bomb technician, told reporters what his thoughts were as he activated the bomb named "Little Boy": "I knew the Japs were in for it, but I felt no particular emotion about it."[77] Parsons kept a log of the flight:

6 August 1945	0245 take-off
0300	started final loading of gun
0315	finished loading
0605	headed for Empire from Iwo
0730	red plugs in (armed the bomb so that it would detonate when released)
0741	started climb. Weather report received that weather over primary and tertiary targets was good but not over secondary target
0838	leveled off at 32,700 feet
0847	electronic fuses were tested and found to be O.K.
0904	course west
0900	Hiroshima in sight
0915 1/2	drop bomb[78]

Hiroshima had not been given any warning. That morning, a weather-observation flight had flown over the city, but this was a regular morning occurrence. People heard an early alert and then an all-clear sound, and they resumed their activities. Then came another plane, followed by the atomic blast.

"A bright light filled the plane," recalled Paul W. Tibbets, the commander. "The first shock wave hit us. We were eleven and a half miles slant from the atomic explosion, but the whole airplane cracked and crinkled." Then the second shock wave hit. "We turned back to look at Hiroshima. The city was hidden by that awful cloud . . . boiling up, mushrooming, terrible and incredibly tall."[79]

"My God!" several crew members exclaimed in horror and wonder.[80] Robert Lewis would never forget what he had witnessed — the evaporation of a city: "Where we had seen a clear city two minutes before, we could now no longer see the city.

We could see smoke and fires creeping up the sides of the mountains."[81]

Viewing the burning city from a distance of eleven miles and an altitude of 29,000 feet, tailgunner George Caron described the scene as a "peep into hell":[82] "The mushroom cloud itself was a spectacular sight, a bubbling mass of purple-gray smoke and you could see it had a red core in it and everything was burning inside. . . . [I]t looked like lava or molasses covering a whole city. . . ."[83]

Meanwhile, on the ground that morning, Naoko Masuoka was on a school trip. She and her friends were singing "Blossoms and buds of the young cherry tree." Around eight o'clock, she heard someone cry out: "A B-29!" "Even as this shout rang in our ears," she said later, "there was a blinding flash and I lost consciousness."[84]

Sanae Kano also remembered seeing a "sudden flash of light." She had been eating breakfast and had her chopsticks in her mouth when it happened. Then there was "a big bang" and she almost fainted. Kano ran out of her house. "At the river, I saw people who were burned black and were crying for water. . . . Some people were in the river drinking the water. The fire wardens were shouting at them telling them that it was dangerous to drink the water. But many people went into the river anyway and drank the water and died. Little children were crying that they were hungry because the bomb fell before they could eat breakfast. I was hungry, too, but I was already a pretty big girl so I didn't cry. A little while later, we were each given two rice balls. Then I fell asleep on the river bank."[85]

After the terrific blast, fires were everywhere. Instantaneously, Hiroshima had been reduced to cinders. People had been burned and were covered with huge blisters. "All green vegetation [had] perished."[86] Yoshiaki Wada found many dead people lying on the bridge. "Some were burned black, some had blistered skin that was peeling off, and some had pieces of glass in them all over."[87]

The force of the explosion had sent millions of shrapnel shards in all directions. Yoshihiro Kimura asked: "Where is mother?" "She is dead," her father answered. Then she noticed that "a nail five inches long had stuck into Mother's head, and she died instantly."[88]

In the chaos of the bomb's aftermath, the survivors experienced other horrors. Iwao Nakamura was thirsty and went to a water tank. "When I got near and was able to see into the tank, I gave an involuntary cry and backed away. What I saw reflected in the blood-stained water were the faces of monsters. They had leaned over the side of the tank and died in that position."[89]

Then, almost as if nature had come to cleanse the burned city, it started to rain hard. The mushroom cloud had carried tons of dirt into the atmosphere; from the sky fell a black rain. "The wind got stronger," Yohko Kuwabara reported, "and it started raining something like ink. This strange rain came down hard out of the gray sky, like a thundershower and the drops stung as if I were being hit by pebbles."[90]

After the rain, the survivors looked around and saw corpses everywhere. "Bodies were cremated every day, in the bamboo grove near the house, on the river bed, or in the corners of fields," Megumi Sera recalled. "It made a horrible smell, and sometimes even the white smoke would come around our house."[91]

Far from this scene of devastation and death, Truman was on board the *Augusta*, returning from Potsdam. On Sunday, August 5, he attended a church service; the next day, Truman and Byrnes decided to have lunch with some crew members. At the beginning of the meal, Truman was suddenly handed a decoded message: "Results clear-cut successful in all respects. Visible effects greater than in any test."[92] Truman was given a map of Japan with Hiroshima circled in red. The city had been bombed four hours earlier. The news he had been anxiously awaiting had arrived, and Truman exclaimed: "This is the greatest thing in history."[93]

In announcing the atomic attack, the president first offered praise to the triumph of American scientists. In language Twain's Hank Morgan would have completely understood, Truman celebrated the bomb as the "greatest marvel" — the achievement of "scientific brains" putting together "infinitely complex pieces of knowledge" with "the capacity of industry to design, and of labor to operate, the machines and methods to do things never done before."[94]

Then Truman went on to hold Japan responsible for its own destruction. "The force from which the sun draws its power," he declared, "has been loosed against those who brought war to the Far East." Truman stated that he had issued the Potsdam ultimatum in order to spare the Japanese people from utter destruction. Demanding immediate unconditional surrender, Truman threatened: "If they do not now accept our terms, they may expect a rain of ruin from the air, the like of which has never been seen on this earth."[95]

Two days later, the Japanese government finally received a full report on the devastation. "When the plane flew over Hiroshima," reported Lieutenant General Seijo Arisue, "there was but one black dead tree, as if a crow was perched over it. There was nothing but that tree. . . . The city itself was completely wiped out."[96]

Hiroshima had been a communications center, a storage area, and an assembly point for troops. But it was not "a purely military" target, as Truman had intended. Of its population of 350,000, 43,000 were soldiers. The United States Strategic Bombing Survey confirmed that only 3,243 troops were killed.[97]

Seventy thousand people were killed instantly, and many more would die — 60,000 by November and another 70,000 by 1950. Most of them would be victims of a new method of killing — radiation. "In Hiroshima, thirty days after the first atomic bomb," wrote Wilfred Burchett of Australia, a reporter who visited the city in September, "people are still dying, mysteriously and horribly — people who were uninjured in the cataclysm from an unknown something which I can only describe as the atomic plague."[98]

On August 8, Russia declared war on Japan. Russia was exactly on schedule: at Yalta, Stalin had agreed that the Soviet Union would enter the war against Japan three months after the end of the conflict in Europe. The Red Army immediately launched a massive attack against Japanese troops in Manchuria; this military action put fierce pressure on Japan to surrender.

A day later, before Japan could fully comprehend the destruction of Hiroshima and respond to the Russian offensive, a plane carrying the second bomb, "Fat Man," took off from Tinian. The target was Kokura, location of war-production plants. But a thick overcast prevented a visual bombing and forced the pilot, Major Charles W. Sweeney, to turn to the secondary target, Nagasaki, a shipbuilding center. Some 70,000 people were killed by the explosion, and another 70,000 died from radiation within five years.

The second atomic attack had been scheduled for August 11, but the timing had been left in the hands of the field commanders, and the date had been moved up two days.

Norman Ramsey, one of the atomic scientists, described how weather conditions had driven the decision to bomb early: "Our original schedule called for take off on the morning of 11 August local time. However, on the evening of 7 August we concluded that we could safely advance the date to August 10.

When we proposed this to Tibbets, he said it was too bad we could not advance the date still another day since good weather was forecast for 9 August with at least five days of bad weather forecast to follow." Thus the plane departed two days ahead of schedule.[99]

Nagasaki would have been spared had the city been bombed as originally scheduled. The Japanese government had not been given sufficient time to respond to the "rain of ruin" that had fallen on Hiroshima and to surrender before another atomic attack. "What we did not take into account," General Marshall admitted years later, ". . . was that the destruction [from the first bomb] would be so complete that it would be an appreciable time before the actual facts of the case would get to Tokyo. The destruction of Hiroshima was so complete that there was no communication at least for a day . . . and maybe longer."[100]

When Emperor Hirohito learned of Hiroshima, he told a loyal associate: "We must bow to the inevitable. No matter what happens to my safety, we must put an end to this war as speedily as possible so that this tragedy will not be repeated." On August 8, he instructed Foreign Minister Shigenori Togo: "Tell Suzuki that the war be ended as soon as possible on the basis of the Potsdam Proclamation." The next day, the Supreme Council for the Direction of the War met, and Togo pleaded with the Council to accept a surrender that included continuation of the emperor system. The Council deadlocked. An extremist faction still wanted to fight to the end.[101]

Late that night, Emperor Hirohito personally intervened. "The time has come," he told them, "when we must bear the unbearable. . . . I swallow my own tears and give my sanction to the proposal to accept the Allied proclamation on the basis outlined by the Foreign Minister." His subjects had no choice but to assent.[102] Hirohito decided to issue an Imperial Rescript, a document sacred to all Japanese, to tell his people that the war had ended. Some of the fanatics forced their way into the palace in order to seize the Rescript, but they failed.

The bomb had generated tremendous political pressure to force Japan to consider surrendering. Marquis Kido later acknowledged: "The presence of the atomic bomb made it easier for us, the politicians, to negotiate peace."[103] However, the Russian declaration of war against Japan was also an important factor. Historian Robert Butow argued that the war was brought to an end by the important combination of two events — the atomic bomb and the Soviet military entry. Together, they created an imperative need to surrender, as well as "a supreme opportunity to turn the tide against the die-hards and to shake the government from the yoke of military oppression."[104]

On August 10, the Japanese government offered to surrender, but only on the condition that the people of Japan be allowed to retain their emperor system. That day, Truman met with his key policymakers, including Secretary of State Byrnes and Chief of Staff William Leahy. The Japanese stipulation infuriated Byrnes, who insisted that the surrender must be "unconditional."[105] But Leahy argued strongly for accepting the Japanese terms. "Some of those around the President wanted to demand his [Hirohito's] execution," he wrote in his memoir, *I Was There.* "If they had prevailed, we might still be at war with Japan. His subjects would probably have fought on until every loyal Japanese was dead. . . ."[106]

Leahy's view prevailed, but in a compromise version. According to his diary entry, Truman "discussed the Jap offer to surrender which came in a couple of hours earlier. They wanted to make a condition precedent to surrender. Our terms are 'conditional.' They wanted to keep the Emperor. We told 'em we'd tell 'em how to keep him, but we'd make the terms."[107] The U.S. statement accepting Japan's surrender, Stimson explained, "implicitly recognized the Emperor's position by prescribing that his power must be subject to the orders of the Allied supreme commander."[108]

In the end, the U.S. allowed Japan to keep its emperor system, and the surrender was not unconditional. "I thought this me-and-God Emperor stuff," a soldier remarked, "was what we were all fighting against." But the news of the peace was welcomed with relief and excitement. "Hell, they can keep the Emperor — and I'll give a couple of officers to boot," an American soldier exclaimed.[109] Another soldier echoed: "I thought it was too good to be true. They should let the people keep Hirohito. Through him we could dictate to the people. They respect him as their God." On August 11, the *New York Times* reported the euphoric reaction with the headline: "GI's in Pacific Go Wild With Joy; 'Let 'Em Keep Emperor,' They Say."[110]

On August 14, Emperor Hirohito told his ministers: "Unless the war be brought to an end at this moment, I fear that the national polity will be destroyed, and the nation annihilated. It is therefore my wish that we bear the unbearable and accept the Allied reply, thus to preserve the state as a state and spare my subjects further suffering."[111]

Peace had come, finally. In Europe, infantry platoon leader Paul Fussell was scheduled to be transferred to the Pacific for the invasion of Japan when he received the news about Hiroshima. "For all the fake manliness of our facades, we cried with relief and joy," he recalled. "We were going to live. We were going to grow up to adulthood after all."[112]

Elliot Johnson had been shipped back to the United States almost immediately after the European war ended and had been told he would be going to the Pacific front. "And I knew, I *knew*," he said later, "that if I went into combat in Japan I would never come back. Most of the guys, the original ones who had been in the unit from the word go, felt that we had used up our luck. We were resentful because we were being sent to

Japan." When Johnson heard the radio announcement about Hiroshima, he felt "enormous relief." "We knew that that effectively spelled the end of World War II, and that we could then be free to go home to our families and resume our lives."[113]

At the battlefronts, soldiers had been singing:

Don't sit under the apple tree with anyone else but me . . .
Don't go walkin' down lover's lane with anyone else but
  me
Till I come marching home.[114]

Now they were finally going home, thanks to the bombing of Hiroshima.

In Seattle, Richard M. Prendergast was getting ready to be shipped to the Pacific for the invasion. "We're sitting on the pier, sharpening our bayonets," he recalled, "when Harry dropped that beautiful bomb. The greatest thing that ever happened. Anybody sitting at the pier at that time would have to agree."[115]

Many children were excited about the end of the war. Their daddies were coming home. Some of them were also awed by the atomic bomb's power to finish the long ordeal so quickly. In a small Indiana town, Janet Sollett recorded in her diary: "The war is over! Completely! Today is V-J Day. . . . Just think, nine days ago people were prepared for a long war but that was before they discovered the Atom Bomb. It is a bomb about the size of a baseball, some say. . . . One of those bombs would completely destroy Elkhart."[116]

At a press conference on August 14, Truman announced that both the United States and Japan had agreed to end the war. The journalists shouted congratulations as they rushed to flash the news. Mrs. Truman and the president then went out to the fountain on the north lawn. At the White House gates, a vast and excited crowd waited for Truman. When he gave them a "V sign in the manner of Churchill," they gave him a great cheer.[117]

The next day, in a letter to his mother, Truman summarized the recent hectic developments: "Since I wrote to you last Tuesday there hasn't been a minute. The speech, the Russian entry into the war, the Japs' surrender offer and the usual business of the President's office have kept me busy night and day. It seems that things are going all right. Nearly every crisis seems to be the worst one but after it's over it isn't so bad."[118]

But, as Truman himself knew, the crisis was not over. He was fully aware of the fact that the United States did not use the atomic bomb *simply* to end the war and thereby save American lives.

4

THE "OVERRIDING CONCERN": TWO SCHOOLS OF THOUGHT

> Having invented a new Holocaust,
> And been the first with it to win a war,
> How they make haste to cry with fingers crossed,
> King's X — no fairs to use it any more!
>
> Robert Frost,
> "U.S. 1946 King's X"[1]

The Coming Cold War

On April 13, the day after he had been sworn in as president, Truman "saw more people that day than anybody in the history of the Presidency up to then." The first person was Secretary of State Edward R. Stettinius. "He told me," Truman recalled, ". . . that Churchill was very upset. The Russians weren't living up to their agreements. And they hadn't been since Yalta."[2]

Ten days later, Truman met with Soviet Foreign Minister Vyacheslav M. Molotov. The president declared that the United States was prepared to carry out all the agreements reached at the February 1945 Yalta Conference, and asked only that the Soviet government do the same. While Truman reaffirmed the American desire for friendship with the Soviet Union, he emphasized that he wanted it understood that this could only be done on a basis of their mutual observation of the agreements and "not on the basis of a one-way street."[3]

By "one-way street," Truman meant the negotiations concerning Poland. Actually, the Yalta agreement itself lacked clarity and precision. Chief of staff Admiral William D. Leahy had been at this conference and taken notes of the discussions. In his memoirs, *I Was There*, Leahy described the agreement's ambiguity on the question of Poland. When he received the report on the new Polish government, Leahy noticed the phrases "strong, free, independent, and democratic Poland," with Russia "guaranteeing" "unfettered elections." Leahy felt that this language was "so susceptible to different interpretations as to promise little toward the establishment of a government in which all the major Polish political parties would be represented." Leahy told Roosevelt: "Mr. President, this is so elastic that the Russians can stretch it all the way from Yalta to Washington without ever technically breaking it." And Roosevelt replied: "I know, Bill — I know it. But it's the best I can do for Poland at this time."[4]

At Yalta, Stalin had explained to Churchill that the Russian people were very concerned about their security. Historically, Poland had been the "corridor" for aggressors to invade Russia. "Twice in the last thirty years," Stalin stressed, "our enemies, the Germans, have passed through this corridor." Poland should be "free, independent in power," able to defend itself against an invasion from Western Europe. To create a strong Poland on the Russian border, Stalin declared, was "not only a question of honor but of life and death for the Soviet state."[5]

However, Stalin had no confidence that an independent Poland would have the power to guard the corridor. The Soviet leader also knew that the Red Army was already in Poland. Roosevelt was aware of this military reality. The United States could do "nothing" to get the Russians to make concessions on Poland, Admiral Leahy wrote. "We would have had to be prepared to take military action to overturn the Soviet *fait accompli*."[6] Stalin knew that Roosevelt had no choice but to recognize that the compromise was "the best" he could do for Poland.

Truman, however, decided he would try to do more for Poland. Shortly after his confrontation with Molotov, Truman received from Stalin what he later described as "one of the most revealing and disquieting messages." Stalin emphatically stated that Russia was determined to secure its borders. The new Polish government, he argued, had to be acceptable to the Soviet Union. Truman saw this as the installation of "a puppet regime of Russia's own making." Therefore, he insisted that the Polish government include Polish democratic leaders who had fled to England.[7]

Truman feared that this disagreement over Poland could lead to a larger conflict between the Soviet Union and the U.S. "The one purpose that dominated me in everything I thought and did [at the time]," Truman wrote in his memoirs, "was to prevent a third world war."[8] This troublesome situation in Europe became what his daughter described as Truman's "overriding concern" — American policy toward Russia.[9] As he worked to bring the war with Japan to an end, Truman found himself giving more and more attention to the threat of Russian expansionism.

Initally, Truman had wanted to cooperate with the Russians in order to help bring peace to the world. The day after he became president, he received a communication from the Russian leader. "Think message from Stalin came in," Truman wrote in his diary, "said he would like to do anything he could to cooperate and I immediately sent him message back. . . ."[10] Truman was not antagonistic toward the Soviet Union, as were men like James Byrnes and Ambassador Averell Harriman.

In his diary on May 10, 1945, Truman recorded his desire to work with the Russians. "I have been trying very carefully to keep all my engagements with the Russians because they are touchy and suspicious of us. . . . But patience I think must be our watchword if we are to have World Peace. To have it we must have the whole-hearted support of Russia, Great Britain and the United States." Truman even seemed to be willing to tolerate the Soviet system of government. On June 7, 1945, he returned to his diary: "I'm not afraid of Russia. They've always been our friends and I can't see any reason why they shouldn't always be." The people in Russia "evidently like their government or they wouldn't die for it. I like ours so let's get along."[11]

But it was already becoming difficult to get along with the Soviet Union. The Polish question had become contentious. Acting Secretary of State Joseph Grew anxiously watched the deterioration of relations between the two allies. On May 19, at 5:00 A.M., he woke up and wrote down his concerns in a private memorandum. He noted that the war had been fought for a defensive purpose. But it would not be "a war to end wars" if it became "merely the transfer of totalitarian dictatorship and power" from Germany and Japan to Soviet Russia. This new arrangement would constitute "as grave a danger to us as did the Axis." Then Grew described Russian expansion in Eastern Europe and Asia. "A future war with Soviet Russia is as certain as anything in this world can be certain."[12]

At this point, the Soviet Union was still an ally, and as Truman prepared for Potsdam, he thought the United States would need Soviet military support in the Pacific war. "Russian entry," the War Department had advised, "will have a profound military effect in that almost certainly it will materially shorten the war and thus save American lives."[13] Truman himself believed that Japan would surrender shortly after the Soviet Union declared war. At a meeting of the Joint Chiefs of Staff on June 18, General George Marshall told Truman: "The impact of Russian entry on the already hopeless Japanese may well be the decisive action levering them into capitulation at that time or shortly thereafter if we land in Japan." Agreeing with this view, Truman realized he had to meet with Stalin at Potsdam in order "to get from Russia all the assistance in the war that was possible."[14]

But Truman did not want to see Stalin just yet. He had promised July 1 as the date for the Potsdam Conference; instead, Truman postponed it until mid-July.[15] He had a hidden reason for the delay. According to the official history of the Atomic Energy Commission, Truman coordinated the Potsdam meeting with the Alamogordo atomic test. In his diary entry for May 21, 1945, former ambassador to Russia Joseph E. Davies wrote that Truman had told him that he "did not want to meet in July. He had his budget (*) on his hands. He also told me of another reason, etc. The test was set for June, but had been postponed until July." The asterisk after "budget" referred to a footnote entry which read: "The atomic bomb. He told me then of the atomic bomb experiment in Nevada [New Mexico]. Charged me with utmost secrecy."[16] On June 6, 1945, Truman told Stimson that he had "postponed" the Potsdam Conference "until the 15th of July on purpose to give us more time."[17]

Manhattan Project director Leslie Groves understood the reason for testing the bomb at that time. "I was extremely anxious to have the test carried off on schedule," he wrote in his memoirs. "One reason for this was that I knew the effect that a successful test would have on the issuance of the Potsdam ultimatum."[18] Los Alamos director J. Robert Oppenheimer recalled: "We were under incredible pressure to get it [the atomic explosion] done before the Potsdam meeting."[19]

The "Quid-Pro-Quo" Strategy

The plan to delay the Potsdam Conference had been suggested to Truman by Secretary of War Henry Stimson. On May 15,

1945, Stimson wrote in his diary: "The trouble is that the President has now promised apparently to meet Stalin and Churchill on the first of July. . . ." Stimson calculated that the atomic bomb would be a dominant factor in the discussions with Stalin, but he knew that the U.S. had not yet perfected the weapon. The secretary of war thought it would be advisable to wait until the experimental bomb had actually been detonated. He referred to the new weapon as a "master card," which he wanted to have "in hand" during the negotiations with Stalin.[20]

Anxious about Russian domination in Eastern Europe and the Soviet challenge in the postwar world, Stimson connected the atomic bomb to diplomacy with Russia. On September 30, 1944, Vannevar Bush and James B. Conant had warned Stimson that American efforts to monopolize the atomic bomb after the war would force Russia to initiate a crash program to develop its own atomic bomb. They predicted that nuclear research would be very rapid in the next five years. To assume the United States would be secure by "holding secret its present atomic knowledge," they cautioned, would be extremely dangerous. It would be "the height of folly," they argued, for the United States and Great Britain to think they would be able to keep their advantage with this new weapon for long. They advised Stimson that the Soviet Union somehow be included in efforts to develop international atomic arms control.[21]

Fearful of a possible atomic arms race with the Soviet Union, Stimson told President Roosevelt in December that they should consider sharing atomic bomb secrets with Russia, but not until they were sure of getting "a real *quid pro quo*" for their "frankness."[22] On March 15, 1945, over lunch at the White House, Stimson returned to this topic when he told Roosevelt that the United States would have to make a decision regarding "the two schools of thought": should we turn atomic technology over to international control, or should we try to maintain our monopoly over atomic technology? This question, Stimson advised Roosevelt, "must be settled before" using the new weapon. "I did not see Franklin Roosevelt again," Stimson wrote, referring to the president's death about a month later, on April 12.[23]

Stimson knew that Truman, as the new president, would have to make a decision about "the two schools of thought." On April 25, he met with Truman to discuss the issue. Within four months, Stimson told the president, we would in "all probability have completed the most terrible weapon ever known in human history, one bomb of which could destroy a whole city." Only the United States at this point controlled the technology and resources to build the bomb. But it was "practically certain" that we would not be able to maintain this monopoly indefinitely. Other nations would sooner or later have the atomic bomb. "The world in its present state of moral advancement compared with its technical development would be eventually at the mercy of such a weapon. In other words, modern civilization might be completely destroyed." The primary question at this point was whether to share atomic technology with other nations, and if so, upon what terms.[24]

As Stimson himself considered the choices, he doubted that an international organization would be workable: "No system of control heretofore considered would be adequate to control this menace."[25] He realized that the Soviet Union was the greatest potential nuclear threat, and that the United States would have to reach some kind of agreement with Russia. On May 16, Stimson explained his concerns to Truman. That evening, the president wrote in his diary: "[Secretary of War Stimson] came in to discuss with me his viewpoint on Russian situation. He has a very sound viewpoint on the subject."[26] In a meeting with Truman on June 6, as preparations were underway for the Potsdam conference, Stimson outlined his "quid pro quo" strategy. In exchange for nuclear secrets, the Russians might agree to be responsive to the "settlement of the Polish, Rumanian, Yugoslavian, and Manchurian problems."[27]

With this advice in mind, Truman went to Potsdam to negotiate with Stalin.

The "Monopoly" Strategy

Truman's overriding focus at the Potsdam Conference was not the waning war with Japan but the looming Soviet threat. In a letter to Bess, July 25, 1945, Truman wrote: "Russia and Poland have gobbled up a big hunk of Germany and want Britain and us to agree. I have flatly refused. We have unalterably opposed the recognition of police governments in the German Axis countries."[28] Negotiations with Stalin were going nowhere; Truman was angry, frustrated. "The persistent way in which Stalin blocked one of the war-preventative measures I had proposed showed how his mind worked and what he was after," Truman complained. "The Russians were planning world conquest." His confrontation with Stalin led Truman to conclude: "Force is the only thing the Russians understand."[29]

While at Potsdam, Truman received the riveting news of the atomic explosion at Alamogordo. "The most secret and the most daring enterprise of the war had succeeded," he wrote in his memoirs. "We were now in possession of a weapon that would not only revolutionize war but could alter the course of history and civilization."[30]

The question, for Truman, was whether to tell Stalin about the bomb. Before departing for Potsdam, Truman had been advised by the Interim Committee that he should inform the Soviet leader about the nuclear project. The committee feared that the failure to be frank on this topic could lead to an atomic arms race. In the judgment of the committee, the U.S. and Russia should discuss the issue of the atomic bomb and its role in the postwar world. This directness would insure that the new technology would become "a substantial aid in preserving the peace of the world rather than a weapon of terror and destruction."[31]

But Truman chose not to be direct with Stalin. During his negotiations with the Russian leader, he "casually" mentioned that the United States had "a new weapon of unusual destructive force." Stalin replied that he was glad to hear the news and added that he hoped the U.S. would make "good use of it against the Japanese."[32]

Stalin already knew about the atomic bomb: his spies had been supplying him with information. He suspected that the United States was also thinking about making "good use" of it to intimidate Russia. After returning to his quarters, Stalin related the conversation to Molotov. The two men noted that Truman had not mentioned the atomic bomb, but they both "guessed at once what he had in mind." "They're raising the price," Molotov commented. Stalin laughed: "Let them. We'll have to talk with Kurchatov today about speeding up our work."[33] Igor V. Kurchatov was in charge of the Soviet nuclear program.[34] Listening to Stalin and Molotov, Marshal G. K. Zhukov realized that "they were talking about the creation of the atomic bomb."[35]

Once Truman held the "master card" of the secret weapon in his hands, he chose not to pursue Stimson's "quid pro quo" strategy with Russia. Instead, he turned to the "monopoly" strategy of keeping the new atomic technology totally under American control.[36] One of the key policymakers promoting this second approach was the secretary of state. Truman regarded Byrnes as an experienced diplomat: he had attended the Yalta Conference and had been respectfully known as the "assistant president" under Roosevelt.[37] As Byrnes and Truman sailed on the *Augusta* on their way to the Potsdam Conference, they had discussed the coming negotiations. In his diary on July 7, Truman wrote: "Had a long talk with my able and conniving Secretary of State. My but he has a keen mind!"[38]

"Conniving" and brilliant, Byrnes had definite ideas about how the U.S. should handle the Soviet threat. As a member of the Interim Committee, Byrnes had been warned by Vannevar Bush and James Conant that the Soviet Union would develop its own bomb in three or four years. But Byrnes estimated that the Russians would take seven to ten years to catch up — a technological lead that would give the United States tremendous diplomatic power.[39] He believed the U.S. should "push ahead" as fast as possible on atomic bomb research and stay ahead.[40]

Byrnes clearly connected the atomic attack on Japan to the need to challenge Soviet expansionism. In his South Carolina home on May 26, Byrnes explained his approach to Leo Szilard. According to Szilard, "Mr. Byrnes did not argue that it was necessary to use the bomb against . . . Japan in order to win the war." But Byrnes was willing to drop the bomb on Japan in order to intimidate Russia. He stated that "our possessing and demonstrating the bomb would make Russia more manageable in Europe." Byrnes pointed out to Szilard that Russian troops had moved into Hungary and Rumania and that it would be difficult to persuade Russia to withdraw them. "The demonstration of the bomb," Byrnes argued, "might impress Russia with America's military might."[41] Two months later, at Potsdam, Byrnes advised Truman that a combat display of the weapon against Japan might be used to bully Russia into submission, and that the bomb "might well put us in a position to dictate our own terms at the end of the war." Byrnes was pushing for a hardline approach — what historian Gar Alperovitz called "atomic diplomacy."[42]

Byrnes's strong-arm strategy toward Russia was already underway in the expansion of the American air war in Europe. Military leaders were aware of the need to demonstrate U.S. military capability to the Soviet leaders. Shortly before the Yalta Conference, General David M. Schlatter had written in his diary: "I feel that our air forces are the blue chips with which we will approach the post-war treaty table, and that [THUNDER-CLAP] will add immeasurably to their strength, or to the Russian knowledge of their strength." "Thunderclap" was the military term for the massive air strikes against Berlin and Dresden.[43] The atomic bomb gave the American military a uniquely powerful weapon that could impress the Russians in a way that would greatly exceed "Thunderclap."

Like Byrnes, General Leslie Groves also believed in the "monopoly" strategy. As director of the Manhattan Project and a guiding force in the Interim Committee, Groves pushed for what he called a "battle test" against Japan. "Already the strategy for the military use of the bomb had been carefully worked out," recalled Arthur Compton of the Interim Committee. "For shaping this strategy General Groves was primarily responsible."[44] The Manhattan Project director knew that Japan was not the only target. "There was never from about two weeks from the time I took charge of this Project," Groves stated, "any illusion on my part but that Russia was our enemy, and the Project was conducted on that basis. I didn't go along with the attitude of the country as a whole that Russia was a gallant ally."[45] Groves believed it would take the Russian scientists ten years or longer to develop their own bomb. During this time, he argued, American policymakers should use this advantage as power diplomacy in dealing with the Russians.

Several other policymakers and scientists, however, saw the bomb's purpose very differently from Byrnes and Groves. They supported the deployment of the bomb against Japan because they hoped that such a combat demonstration would frighten everyone into cooperating to control this terrifying new force. "Unless the bomb were used [against Japan]," observed Harvey H. Bundy of the Interim Committee, "it would be impossible to persuade the world that the saving of civilization in the future would depend on a proper international control of atomic energy."[46]

Similarly, Los Alamos Weapons Laboratory director and Interim Committee adviser J. Robert Oppenheimer wanted to deploy the bomb in order to insure world peace. He told Szilard that we should inform the Russians about our atomic bomb and that we were planning to use it against Japan. This information would compel the Russians to cooperate with us in establishing controls for the new weapon. However, Szilard doubted that this strategy would work. "Well," Oppenheimer replied, "don't you think that if we tell the Russians what we intend to do and then use the bomb in Japan, the Russians will understand it?" Szilard countered: "They'll understand it only too well."[47] Oppenheimer thought that one of the "overriding considerations" for dropping the bomb on Japan was the effect it would have on "the stability of the postwar world."[48]

Interim Committee members James Conant and Arthur Compton also believed that the bomb could be used as an alarm, a firebell in the night. Conant advised Stimson that "the bomb *must be used*," for it was "the only way to awaken the world to the necessity of abolishing war altogether. No technological demonstration, even if it had been possible under the conditions of war — which it was not — could take the place of the actual use with its horrible results."[49]

Compton rationalized the bomb as a force for good. "What a tragedy it was that this power should become available first in time of war and that it must first be used for human destruction," he wrote in his autobiography. "If, however, it would result in the shortening of the war and the saving of lives — if it would mean bringing us closer to the time when war would be abandoned as a means of settling international disputes — here must be our hope and our basis for courage." Indeed, as a ghastly warning to the entire world, the bomb could help put an end to war. Compton told Stimson: "If the bomb were not used in the present war, the world would have no adequate warning as to what was to be expected if war should break out again."[50]

In the minds of many atomic scientists, a combat demonstration of the new weapon could greatly benefit future generations. Edward Teller believed that we needed to convince the world that the next war would be unbearably destructive. "For this purpose," he argued, "actual combat-use might even be the best thing."[51]

While the atomic strategy against Japan was linked to long-term objectives in the postwar world, it was also connected to specific geopolitical concerns in Asia related to Russian expansion. Policymakers were aware of the Russian promise at Yalta to enter the war against Japan three months after Germany's surrender on May 7. The U.S. invasion of Japan, however, was scheduled for November 1. By then, Russia would have declared war against Japan and would have leverage at the peace table. Everything depended on the atomic bomb test scheduled for July 16.

"Neither the President nor I," Byrnes said, "were anxious to have them [the Russians] enter the war after we had learned of this successful test."[52] The atomic bomb meant that the U.S. no longer needed Russian military assistance to defeat Japan. In fact, Russian armed intervention would threaten American postwar interests. "Once Russia is in the war against Japan," Acting Secretary of State Joseph Grew wrote in his diary on May 19, "then Mongolia, Manchuria, and Korea will gradually slip into Russia's orbit, to be followed in due course by China and

eventually Japan. . . ." The situation in Asia was extremely volatile. Concerned about Soviet demands for "concessions" in that
region, Stimson informed Grew that Russia had the military
power to obtain them "regardless of U.S. military action short
of war."[53] He meant war against the Soviet Union.

August 8, the date for Soviet entry into the war, was approaching rapidly.[54] Truman received reports that Russian
troops were massing at the Manchurian border.

Stalin, on the other hand, feared that the war might end before Russia could enter it. He wanted to have bargaining power
at the peace table. "Stalin was leaning on our officers to start
military actions as soon as possible," Nikita Khrushchev recalled. "Stalin had his doubts about whether the Americans
would keep their word. . . . What if Japan capitulated before
we entered the war? The Americans might say, we don't owe
you anything."[55] On August 9, a 1.5-million-strong Red Army
moved against Japanese forces in Manchuria.

At Yalta, Stalin had stated his terms for Russian participation
in the war against Japan. They included communist rule in
Outer Mongolia and its independence from China, Soviet recov-
ery of southern Sakhalin, which had been ceded in the Russo-
Japanese war of 1904–5, and annexation of the Kurile Islands.
"I only want to have returned to Russia," Stalin told Roosevelt
at Yalta, "what the Japanese have taken from my country." The
president said: "That seems like a very reasonable suggestion
from our ally — they only want to get back that which has been
taken from them."[56] Furthermore, Stalin remembered Japanese
past aggression against Russia and was determined to protect
his nation's eastern border. The Soviet leader wanted to be sure
that Japan would not endanger the Soviet Union again. "One
should keep Japan vulnerable from all sides, north, west, south,
east," Stalin declared, "then she will keep quiet."[57]

After the successful Alamogordo atomic explosion, Truman

and key policymakers like Byrnes sought to thwart Stalin's ambitions in Asia. The war against Japan had to be brought to an
end as soon as possible, or the Soviet Union would have powerful influence in China and even in postwar Japan. According
to Secretary of the Navy James Forrestal, "Byrnes said he was
most anxious to get the Japanese affair over with before the
Russians got in."[58] The use of the atomic bomb, Byrnes believed,
would force Japan to surrender quickly and prevent Soviet domination in China. The Soviet violations of the Yalta agreement
in Poland, Rumania, and Bulgaria had persuaded Byrnes that
he would rather not have the Soviet Union enter the war against
Japan. "Notwithstanding Japan's persistent refusal to surrender
unconditionally," Byrnes recounted in his autobiography, "I believed the atomic bomb would be successful and would force
the Japanese to accept surrender on our terms. I feared what
would happen when the Red Army entered Manchuria."[59]

Even the selection of targets in Japan was influenced by concerns over the presence of Russian power in Asia. On the original list of Japanese cities to be bombed was Kyoto. Stimson had
visited this beautiful city in the 1920s and did not want a city
of such great cultural and religious significance destroyed. Stimson appreciated Japanese art, but in his plea to Truman to save
Kyoto, he advanced a practical and political argument. The
atomic bombing of Kyoto would leave the Japanese people even
more bitter toward America, he pointed out, and the U.S.
should try to keep a path open to reconciliation with Japan.
The United States would need Japan as an ally in Asia in the
event of Russian aggression in Manchuria.

The news of the atomic bombing of Hiroshima produced
shock in Moscow. "[It] had an acutely depressing effect on everybody," reported Alexander Werth, the London *Sunday Times*
correspondent in Moscow at the time. "It was clearly realized
that this was a New Fact in the world's power politics, that the

bomb constituted a threat to Russia, and some Russian pessimists I talked to that day dismally remarked that Russia's desperately hard victory over Germany was now 'as good as wasted.' "[60]

The combat demonstration in Japan did not lead to Soviet cooperation in the international control of atomic weapons. What followed instead was the acceleration of the atomic arms race. Twenty-four hours after the bombing of Hiroshima, Stalin summoned five of the leading Soviet nuclear scientists and ordered them to catch up with the United States "in the minimum of time, regardless of cost."[61] On August 22, the director of military intelligence in Moscow cabled the head of a Soviet spy ring: "Take measures to organize acquisition of documentary materials on the atomic bomb! The technical process, drawings, calculations."[62] A month later, Moscow sent instructions to speed up the mining of uranium in Central Asia.

On September 23, 1949, Truman announced that the Soviet Union had successfully exploded its first atomic bomb — Joe I.

5

REMEMBERING PEARL HARBOR

He had been so close to it, caught up in it for so long that its simplicity struck him deep inside his chest; Trinity Site, where they exploded the first atomic bomb, was only three hundred miles to the southeast at White Sands. . . . From the jungles of his dreaming he recognized why the Japanese voices had merged with Laguna voices . . . the lines of cultures and worlds were drawn in flat dark lines on fine light sand, converging in the middle of witchery's final ceremonial sand painting. From that time on, human beings were one clan again, united by the fate the destroyers had planned for them, for all living things; united by a circle of death that devoured people in cities twelve thousand miles away, victims who had never known these mesas, who had never seen the delicate colors of rocks which boiled up their slaughter.

Leslie Marmon Silko,
Ceremony[1]

The "Day of Infamy"

Two days after Japan's attack on Pearl Harbor, Roosevelt held a fireside chat with the American people. In a world ruled by international gangsters, he said, isolationism had endangered the United States. Now the country had been forced into the war. "We don't like it — we didn't want to get in it —

but we are in it and we're going to fight it with everything we've got."[2]

Japan's devastating surprise attack on Pearl Harbor sent waves of shock across America. A fierce American rage demanded revenge for this "treacherous" action. The bitterness over Pearl Harbor aroused a national bloodthirstiness that seemed unquenchable until the enemy had been totally vanquished. Driven by this singular focus, Admiral William Halsey, commander of the South Pacific Force, gave his men a direct and simple message: "Kill Japs, kill Japs, kill more Japs."[3] A motto of the U.S. Marines urged: "Remember Pearl Harbor — keep 'em dying."[4] General Joseph Stilwell wrote to his wife: "When I think of how these bowlegged cockroaches have ruined our calm lives it makes me want to wrap Jap guts around every lamppost in Asia."[5]

In the wake of Pearl Harbor, the bloody battles in the Pacific intensified an American desire for violent vengeance. "Never before has the nation fought a war in which our troops so hate the enemy and want to kill him," a reporter for *Newsweek* wrote in January 1945. "This intense hatred was first aroused by the sneak attack on Pearl Harbor. From then on it was fed by countless small incidents of dirtiness and treachery. I remember men who, when they came to the Pacific, had no particular hatred of or desire to kill Japanese. Then they saw their buddies machine gunned while parachuting from a plane or killed by a hand grenade some wounded Jap held under his armpit and detonated when an American bent down to help him. When treachery like that affects you, or somebody you know, you grow to hate violently."[6]

The ferocious memories of Pearl Harbor, Bataan, Iwo Jima, Luzon, Okinawa, and other battles set a course that would lead to the bombing of Hiroshima. Arthur Compton, head of the Chicago Metallurgical Laboratory, recounted what a young physicist at Los Alamos had said during the war: "I have buddies who have fought through the battle of Iwo Jima. Some of them have been killed, others wounded. We've got to give these men the best weapons we can produce. If one of these men should be killed because we didn't let them use the [atomic] bombs, I would have failed them. I just could not make myself feel that I had done my part."[7]

After the war, a poll conducted by *Fortune* in December 1945 found that 54 percent of the respondents approved of the bombing of Hiroshima and Nagasaki. Twenty-three percent of the respondents agreed that the U.S. "should have quickly used many more of them [atomic bombs] before Japan had a chance to surrender."[8] In a telegram sent to President Truman after the atomic bombing of Hiroshima, Senator Richard B. Russell of Georgia urged: "If we do not have available sufficient number of atomic bombs with which to finish the job immediately, let us carry on with TNT and fire bombs until we can produce them."[9]

The Racialization of the Pacific War

Shortly after the atomic attack on Hiroshima, the *Philadelphia Inquirer* printed a cartoon that depicted a brute resembling an ape staring blankly upward at an exploding atomic bomb.[10] The image of the Japanese as "apes" reflected the ways the Pacific conflict became what historian John Dower termed a "war without mercy."[11] In this violent struggle, both Japan and the United States, respectively, had racialized the enemy.

Urging Asia to unite in a race war against white America, Japan sought to arouse Chinese antagonism toward the United States. Japanese propaganda condemned U.S. law restricting immigration from China. Tokyo radio broadcasts directed at China described how the Chinese in the United States suffered from "a campaign of venomous vilification of the character of the Chinese people." Tokyo warned on the air waves: "Far from waging this war to liberate the oppressed peoples of the world, the Anglo-American leaders are trying to restore the obsolete system of imperialism."[12]

While Japan's leaders condemned Anglo-American expansionism, they had been promoting their own version of imperialism. At the beginning of the twentieth century, Japan colonized Korea and established a brutally repressive regime. During the 1930s, Japan invaded China and waged a vicious military campaign against Chinese resistance. In China, Japanese soldiers showed total disrespect for international laws on warfare. Atrocities were pervasive. During the 1937 "Rape of Nanking," Japanese soldiers massacred several hundred thousand Chinese. In a murderous and cruel rampage against civilians, they raped, bayonetted, and beheaded their victims. Japan was determined to create a Greater East Asia Co-Prosperity Sphere by barbaric force as well as racial propaganda.

Japanese racial ideology was rooted in their mythology and culture. The Japanese people, according to this view, belonged to the superior "Yamato race." "There are superior and inferior races in the world," declared Japanese political leader Chikuhei Nakajima in 1940, "and it is the sacred duty of the leading race to lead and enlighten the inferior ones." Pure-blooded and descended from the gods, he argued, the Japanese were "the sole superior race in the world."[13]

In their war against the United States, the Japanese people were told by their leaders that they had a glorious mission. Their responsibility, stated Foreign Minister Yosuke Matsuoka, was "to prevent the human race from becoming devilish, to rescue it from destruction and lead it to the world of light." A uniquely "pure" race, the Japanese had to fight against the "brutes," "wild beasts," monsters, devils, and demons of

America and Europe. The Japanese dehumanized the enemy in what they considered a race war: they portrayed the Americans as "hairy, twisted-nosed savages." War propaganda condemned "the Bestial American People," and urged soldiers: "Beat the Americans to Death!" Thus, Japan had defined the conflict as an all-out war to exorcise and totally destroy the demons. "Exterminist logic," historian Dower noted sadly, "was not an English or American monopoly."[14] This logic led Japanese soldiers to commit atrocities against captured American troops. The most shocking incident occurred at Corregidor. At this outpost in 1942, 76,000 American and Filipino defenders surrendered to the Japanese; during the forced trek to the stockades, 7,000 POWs died, most of them brutally murdered in what would be called the Bataan Death March.

Meanwhile, on this side of the Pacific, the United States was defining the Japanese enemy as demons, savages, subhumans, and beasts. Comic books portrayed the Japanese as "loathsome buck-toothed little yellow savages, but cunning devils."[15] In July, *Time* magazine declared: "The ordinary unreasoning Jap is ignorant. Perhaps he is human. Nothing . . . indicates it."[16]

Such racial stereotyping, however, did not develop in the U.S. war against Germany. Earlier, during World War I, the enemy was denounced as "Huns," but during World War II, the enemy was Hitler and the Nazis, not the German people. "They looked like us," thought many white Americans.[17] Indeed, many Americans were of German ancestry. Except for the English, the Germans constituted the largest group of immigrants in America. On the other hand, white Americans viewed the Japanese as aliens, as the "Other." The Japanese did not look like them. "The war against the Japanese became a kind of racist fight," recalled James Covert, whose father and brother had fought in the armed forces, "whites against the yellow race, and the yellow races were inferior. In Europe it was a little different.

You felt that Europeans were good people. They just followed the wrong leaders."[18] Lapel buttons depicted the enemy differently. A button for the German enemy showed a picture of Hitler, with the words "Wanted for Murder." A button for the Japanese stated "Jap Hunting License — Open Season — No Limit."[19] Atrocities in the European war were usually depicted as "Nazi" crimes, committed by evil Germans like Hitler. On the other hand, the enemy in the Pacific was invariably described simply as the "Japs." Unlike the Germans, the Japanese were assigned simian images: they were gorillas, "yellow apes," and "yellow monkeys." As he ordered his men to go into battle against the Japanese, an American admiral urged his men to go and "get some more Monkey meat."[20]

Sometimes, perhaps often, American soldiers literally followed such urgings. "You developed an attitude of no mercy because they [the Japanese] had no mercy on us," recalled E. B. Sledge. "It was a no-quarter kind of thing. . . . I've seen guys shoot Japanese wounded when it really was not necessary and knock gold teeth out of their mouths. . . . One of my buddies carried a bunch of 'em in a sock. . . . The way you extracted gold teeth was by putting the tip of the blade on the tooth of the dead Japanese — I've seen guys do it to wounded ones — and hit the hilt of the knife to knock the tooth loose."[21] A marine was excited about taking teeth: "They say the Japs have a lot of gold teeth. I'm going to make myself a necklace."[22]

Many American soldiers collected other grisly battlefield trophies — scalps, skulls, bones, and ears. One of them said: "I'm going to bring back some Jap ears. Pickled."[23] As a soldier in the Pacific, Robert Lekachman recalled that he "didn't collect ears [of dead Japanese soldiers]." But he "knew some others did. We had been fed tales of these yellow thugs, subhumans, with teeth that resembled fangs. If a hundred thousand Japs were killed, so much the better. Two hundred thousand, even better."[24]

Historian Dower reported that "most fighting men had personal knowledge of such practices and accepted them as inevitable under the circumstances." Comparing the Pacific war with the European war, he continued: "It is virtually inconceivable, however, that teeth, ears, and skulls could have been collected from German or Italian war dead and publicized in the Anglo-American countries without provoking an uproar; and in this we have yet another inkling of the racial dimensions of the war."[25]

The taking of war trophies, especially scalps, was a legacy of an earlier racialized war — the winning of the West. Many of the soldiers and their commanders had fathers and grandfathers who had fought against Indians. In an essay, "How We Felt About the War," published shortly after the end of the conflict, historian Allan Nevins observed: "Probably in all our history, no foe has been so detested as were the Japanese." He located the fierce fighting within the context of American westward expansion: "Emotions forgotten since our most savage Indian wars were awakened by the ferocities of Japanese commanders."[26] The Pacific islands had become America's "frontier." "When I was a young boy," a soldier said, "we always played cowboys and Indians, and when I landed on Guadalcanal that's what I felt like — I was playing a game, it was not real. Even though I knew it was real. . . ." Another soldier described the Japanese attackers as "whooping like a bunch of wild Indians."[27] Jungle combat against Japanese soldiers was often characterized as "Indian fighting," and the perimeter outside U.S. military control was called "Indian country."[28] Commenting on the fighting skills of Japanese soldiers, Colonel Milton A. Hill stated that the "Japs" were "good at infiltration, too; as good as Indians ever were."[29] Recycling an old frontier adage, Admiral Halsey declared: "The only good Jap is a Jap who's been dead six months."[30]

Clearly, the American war in the Pacific was rooted deeply in our country's past.

Hiroshima: The Crucible of Race in American History

From the very beginning of what would become the United States, race has been a significant influence. After the founding of Jamestown in 1607, the English colonists often stereotyped the Indians as "savages" and "cruel beasts." They seized Indian lands, and when they encountered resistance, they sometimes engaged in total war against the Indians. "Victory may be gained in many ways," a colonist declared in 1622: "by force, by surprise, by famine in burning their Corn, by destroying and burning their Boats, Canoes, and Houses . . . by pursuing and chasing them with our horses, and blood-hounds to draw after them, and mastives to tear them." As the English fought the Indians and appropriated their lands, they began to racialize the "savagery" of the Indians. This occurred particularly in New England, where the colonists viewed the "Tawny" people as "devils," doomed to what Increase Mather called "utter extirpation." This view justified the mass killing of Indians. After a bloody battle against the Pequots in Connecticut in 1637, an English officer wrote: "Many were burnt in the fort, both men, women, and children. . . . There were about four hundred souls in this fort, and not above five of them escaped out of our hands." Commander John Mason explained that God had pushed the Pequots into a "fiery oven," "filling the place with dead bodies."[31]

Meanwhile, Africans had been introduced into the English colonies in the seventeenth century, and the institution of slavery was established. Their presence, however, threatened the view of America as a white society. In the eighteenth century, this problem led Thomas Jefferson to advocate the abolition of slavery. The owner of over two hundred slaves, the author of the Declaration of Independence felt guilty for appropriating their labor and liberty. Slavery, he also noticed, had created anti-white resentment and hatred among blacks, and he feared a future of race wars in America. Jefferson thought blacks might be naturally inferior in intelligence, and he was worried about the rapid increase of the black population — what he called "this blot in our country."[32] Jefferson had a plan for the "emancipation and expatriation" of the slaves. Black infants, he proposed, would be taken from their mothers and trained in industrious occupations until they had reached a proper age for deportation to Santo Domingo. In this way, "the old stock" of blacks would die off naturally and finally disappear.[33]

In 1801, two years before President Jefferson negotiated the Louisiana Purchase, he informed James Monroe that he looked forward to the time when the American continent would be covered with "a same people speaking the same language, governed in similar forms, and by similar laws."[34] Earlier, Congress had defined who could be members of such "a same people." In 1790, the lawmakers passed a law specifying that in order to be eligible for naturalized citizenship, a person would have to be "white."[35]

One of the reasons for this racial requirement was a new political idea that had been forged in the American Revolution — democracy. This principle was based on the belief that the citizens of the new nation were the source of the government's authority. The government would guarantee the natural rights of life, liberty, and the pursuit of happiness; in turn, individual citizens would be self-governing. Many leaders of the new republic believed that citizens needed to be intelligent in order to exercise political responsibility, and therefore they would have to be "white" — citizens composed of "a same people."

This idea of democracy often embraced an expansionist vision for the new nation. The continent, Jefferson thought, offered an abundance of uncultivated land. Thus, Americans would be able to pursue their dream of democracy so long as there were "vacant lands." "When we get piled upon one another in large cities as in Europe," he warned, "we shall become corrupt as in Europe, and go to eating one another as they do there." The very success of the democratic experiment depended on continuous expansion westward.[36]

By the end of the nineteenth century, however, the continent was nearly "covered" with Americans: they had reached the Pacific and were settling across this vastness called America. In 1891, the United States census superintendent announced that the frontier had come to an end. Two years later, the young historian Frederick Jackson Turner reflected on the meaning of this new development in a paper entitled "The Significance of the Frontier in American History." He noted that American democracy had been born on the frontier — "the meeting point between savagery and civilization." Whites had advanced the frontier and had won the West by "a series of Indian wars." But he wondered: what would happen to democracy in a frontierless America, where there was no more "free land"? Turner assured Americans: "He would be a rash prophet who should assert that the expansive character of American life has now entirely ceased. . . . Movement has been its dominant fact, and, unless this training [of the frontier experience] has no effect upon a people, the American intellect will continually demand a wider field for its exercise."[37]

By then, that "wider field" had already been extended to Asia. In 1853, Commodore Matthew C. Perry had sailed his armed naval ships into Tokyo Bay and forcefully opened Japan's doors to the West. About the same time, American ships had reached China and had begun transporting Chinese immigrants east to America.

The Chinese immigrants were needed as laborers in the growing economy of the West, and by 1870 there were 63,000 of them in the United States. Though they were wanted as workers, however, they were despised because of their race. White workers referred to the Chinese as "nagurs" ["niggers"], and a magazine cartoon in California depicted a Chinese as a bloodsucking vampire with slanted eyes, a pigtail, dark skin, and thick lips. Many whites likened the Chinese to blacks — heathen, morally inferior, and savage.[38] In the 1854 decision of *People v. Hall,* the California Supreme Court declared that the words "Indian, Negro, Black, and White" were "generic terms, designating races," and that therefore "Chinese and other people not white" could not testify against whites.[39] In 1882, Congress did something unprecedented: it passed the Chinese Exclusion Act. For the first time, the United States restricted immigration based on race.

Ironically, the Statue of Liberty was erected three years later. France had given the monument to the United States as a symbol of friendship and liberty. Americans had to raise $280,000 to pay for the construction of the pedestal, and they were asked to make contributions. When a Chinese immigrant was solicited for a donation, he exploded in protest. In a letter to the *American Missionary* in 1885, Saum Song Bo angrily wrote: "A paper was presented to me yesterday for inspection, and I found it to be specially drawn up for subscription among my fellow countrymen toward the Pedestal Fund of the Bartholdi Statue of Liberty. Seeing that the heading is an appeal to American citizens, to their love of country and liberty, I feel that my countrymen and myself are honored in being thus appealed to as citizens for the cause of liberty. But the word liberty makes me think of the fact that this country is the land of liberty for men of all nations except the Chinese."[40]

The Chinese seemed to be particularly threatening: they were viewed as a "yellow peril." Coming to America in increasing numbers, they were perceived by many whites as an invading army — the yellow hordes of a modern Genghis Khan, the frightening specter of Europe in the thirteenth century. In 1882, in his fantasy entitled *Short and True History of the Taking of California and Oregon by the Chinese in the Year A. D. 1899*, Robert Wolters pictured a nightmarish Chinese military conquest of the West Coast.[41] Again, twenty-five years later, Marsden Manson portrayed a conflict between China and the U.S. in *The Yellow Peril in Action*.[42]

The 1882 Chinese Exclusion Act successfully stemmed the flow of Chinese immigrants, but shortly afterward, a new "yellow peril" seemed to loom on the horizon: immigrants from Japan began coming to America.

This new immigration was also linked to American expansion into Asia. Commodore Perry's 1853 intrusion had ignited dynamic developments within Japan. As Japanese leaders watched Western powers colonizing China, they worried that Japan would be the next victim. In 1868, they restored the Meiji Emperor and began establishing a strong centralized government with a dual strategy — industrialization and militarization. To finance this program, the Japanese government imposed high taxes on farmers; facing economic difficulties, tens of thousands of them emigrated to the United States, beginning in the 1880s. By 1920, some 200,000 Japanese had gone to Hawaii, and another 180,000 to the American mainland.

These Japanese immigrants experienced harsh discrimination, especially in California. Racist curses stung their ears: "Jap Go Home." "Goddamn Jap!" "Yellow Jap!" "Dirty Jap!" Ugly graffiti assaulted their eyes at railroad stations and in restrooms: "Japs Go Away!" "Fire the Japs!"[43] On the street corners in Los Angeles, scribblings on the sidewalks threatened: "Japs, we do not want you." Outside a small town in the San Joaquin Valley, a sign on the highway warned "No More Japs Wanted Here."[44]

This discrimination went beyond words. "People even spit on Japanese in the streets," Juhei Kono told an interviewer. "In fact, I myself, was spit upon more than a few times." "There was so much anti-Japanese feeling in those days!" exclaimed Choichi Nitta. "They called us 'Japs' and threw things at us. When I made a trip to Marysville to look for land, someone threw rocks."[45] In the cities, they were pelted with stones, and their businesses were vandalized — their store windows smashed and the sidewalks in front smeared with horse manure. At theaters, the Japanese were often refused admittance or seated in a segregated section. "I went to a theatre on Third Avenue with my wife and friends," an immigrant recalled. "We were all led up to the second balcony with the Blacks." Entering barbershops operated by whites, Japanese were told: "We don't cut animal's hair." The Japanese also faced residential segregation. When the newcomers tried to rent or buy houses, they were turned down by realtors, who explained: "If Japanese live around here, then the price of the land will go down." The Japanese immigrants were socially shunned and geographically isolated in rural areas and Japantowns.[46]

They were also attacked politically. In 1904, the American Federation of Labor called for the prohibition of Japanese immigration. The labor union explained that the newcomers from Japan lacked the capacity to be part of the American labor movement. They did not share the white workers' "God," their "hopes, their ambitions, their love of this country." The Japanese could not become "union men" because they were unassimilable.[47]

In San Francisco, white workers initiated a political campaign for Japanese exclusion. Demanding the renewal of the Chinese Exclusion Act scheduled to expire in 1902, white workers urged Congress to extend the ban to the Japanese. In 1901, Governor Henry Gage warned that the unrestricted immigration of Japanese laborers constituted a "menace" to American labor similar to the earlier "peril from Chinese labor." Under Governor Gage's leadership, the legislature sent Congress a petition demanding Japanese exclusion. Four years later, white workers formed the Asiatic Exclusion League. "The Caucasian and Asiatic races are unassimilable," they stated in their constitution. "The preservation of the Caucasian race upon American soil . . . necessitates the adoption of all possible measures to prevent or minimize the immigration of Asiatics to America."[48]

On October 11, 1906, the San Francisco Board of Education directed school principals to send "all Chinese, Japanese and Korean children to the Oriental School." This segregation policy sent waves of indignation across the Pacific. The government of Japan quickly sent a protest to Washington, angrily claiming that the school board action violated a treaty provision guaranteeing Japanese children in the United States equal educational opportunities.[49]

The action of the school board precipitated an international crisis. President Theodore Roosevelt had respect as well as concern for Japan's military power: in 1905, Japan had decisively won the war against Russia. Anxious to avoid a confrontation between the United States and Japan, Roosevelt invited Mayor Eugene Schmitz and the members of the school board to Washington.

The school board was actually trying to create an incident in order to pressure the federal government to restrict immigration from Japan. There were only 93 Japanese students in San Francisco, an insignificant number to place in a segregated school. Roosevelt and the school board reached a compromise. Emerging from their discussions with the president, the officials stated: "We have every reason to believe that the administration now shares, and that it will share, our way of looking at the problem, and that the result we desire — the cessation of the immigration of Japanese laborers, skilled or unskilled, to this country, will be speedily achieved." Satisfied by assurances from the president, the school board members returned to San Francisco and rescinded the segregation order, "excepting in so far as it applied to Chinese and Korean children." President Roosevelt, in turn, entered into negotiations with Japan to limit Japanese immigration. Under the terms of the 1908 Gentlemen's Agreement, Roosevelt extracted an understanding that Japan would limit Japanese immigration.[50]

Many whites in California, however, wanted not only to restrict Japanese immigration but also to impose discriminatory legislation on the Japanese already there. In 1913, the California legislature passed a law designed to deny landownership to Japanese immigrants. While the law did not specifically refer to the Japanese, it was aimed at them. Referring to the 1790 Naturalization Act, the new law declared unlawful the ownership of "real property" by "aliens ineligible to citizenship."[51] Similiar laws were also enacted in Washington, Arizona, Oregon, Idaho, Nebraska, Texas, Kansas, Louisiana, Montana, New Mexico, Minnesota, and Missouri.

These restrictive land laws were based on the ineligibility of the Japanese to naturalized citizenship. Actually, however, their status as it related to citizenship was not completely clear. The 1790 law had granted naturalized citizenship to "white" immigrants only, and the 1882 law had explicitly withheld this privilege from the Chinese. But the laws did not specifically exclude Japanese, and, consequently, several hundred Japanese immigrants had been able to secure citizenship in the lower federal courts. This practice came to an end in 1906, when the United States attorney general ordered the federal courts to deny naturalized citizenship to Japanese aliens.[52]

Japanese immigrants protested this ruling, and one of them took his case to court. Determined to prove his fitness for citizenship, Takao Ozawa filed an application for U.S. citizenship in 1914. He was confident he was qualified. After arriving in California in 1894, he had graduated from high school and then studied at the University of California, Berkeley, for three years. But Ozawa's application was denied. He then challenged the denial in court; in 1916, a U.S. District Court ruled that Ozawa was not eligible for naturalized citizenship because he was not "white." Ozawa appealed to the United States Supreme Court. He informed the Court that he was "at heart a true American." He did not have any connection with the Japanese government or with any Japanese churches or organizations. His family went to an American church and his children attended American schools. He said that he spoke the "American [English] language at home." In 1922, the Supreme Court held that Ozawa was not entitled to naturalized citizenship because he was "clearly . . . not Caucasian."[53]

Two years later, Congress enacted a general immigration law that included a provision prohibiting the entry of aliens ineligible to citizenship. Although not named explicitly, the Japanese had been singled out for special discriminatory treatment, for the Chinese and the Asian Indians had already been excluded by other legislation. The anti-Japanese exclusionists gave their reasons for this legislation. In his testimony to Congress shortly before its passage, newspaper editor V. S. McClatchy of California declared: "Of all races ineligible to citizenship, the Japanese are the least assimilable and the most dangerous to this country. . . . With great pride of race, they have no idea of assimilating in the sense of amalgamation. They do not come to this country with any desire or any intent to lose their racial or national identity. They come here specifically and professedly for the purpose of colonizing and establishing here permanently the proud Yamato race. They never cease to be Japanese."[54]

In a "Message from Japan to America," the *Japan Times and Mail* protested against the new law: If the restrictionist measure had excluded all immigration or had placed Japan on the same basis as other nations, Japan would not have resented it. "But Japan does resent a clause that, while not mentioning Japanese specifically, affects Japanese alone of all the races . . . and stamps Japanese as of an inferior race."[55] In an editorial on the 1924 law, a Japanese-American newspaper warned that Congress had "planted the seeds" of possible future "cataclysmic racial strife" by "branding" the Japanese people inferior.[56]

Condemning the new law as discrimination based on race, the Japanese government explained the reasons for the Japanese reluctance to assimilate: "The process of assimilation can thrive only in a genial atmosphere of just and equitable treatment. Its natural growth is bound to be hampered under such a pressure of invidious discriminations as that to which Japanese residents in some states of the American Union have been subjected, at law and in practice, for nearly twenty years. It seems hardly fair to complain of the failure of foreign elements to merge in a community, while the community chooses to keep them apart from the rest of its membership."[57] Racism had forced the Japanese immigrants to live segregated lives in America, rendering it impossible for them to feel at home in their adopted country.

Beneath racial discrimination and exclusion was a deeper fear of the Japanese: they also seemed to represent a military threat to America. The immigrants were seen as the advance guard of an invasion from Japan. In an editorial entitled "Yellow Peril," published on March 11, 1905, *Organized Labor* warned its readers that the Japanese government was spying in the United States and had plans of conquest: its goal was to make California "its Manchurian fields."[58]

Three years later, in *The Valor of Ignorance,* Homer Lea offered a scary scenario of Japan first occupying the Philippines and then invading the West Coast of the United States. According to historian Dower, Lea was "an unabashed example of a white supremacist who feared that Anglo-Saxon purity was threatened by rot within as well as enemies at the gate."[59] A guardian of America's gate, Lea urged the country to prepare militarily for a race war with Japan.[60] Lea's book went out of print, but, as historian Roger Daniels noted, it was reissued with "much fanfare shortly after Pearl Harbor."[61] In fact, it was published by the prestigious Harper & Brothers, with an introduction by Clare Boothe Luce, wife of the publisher of *Time, Life,* and *Fortune.*[62]

One of Lea's readers was Secretary of War Henry Stimson. In his diary on February 10, 1942, he wrote: "In those days [Lea's] book seemed fantastic. Now the things that he prophesied seem quite possible."[63]

The Internment of Japanese Americans

In the very same diary entry for that day, Stimson also recorded that President Roosevelt was preparing to issue an executive order for the mass removal and internment of Japanese Americans on the West Coast. "The second generation Japanese," Stimson wrote, "can only be evacuated either as part of a total evacuation, giving access to the areas only by permits, or by frankly trying to put them out on the ground that their racial characteristics are such that we cannot understand or trust even the citizen Japanese. This latter is the fact but I am afraid it will make a tremendous hole in our constitutional system to apply it."[64] The winds of war hysteria and racism in California were blowing America into that very "hole" in our country's democratic fabric.

Shortly after he inspected the still-smoking ruins at Pearl Harbor, Navy Secretary Frank Knox issued a statement to the press: "I think the most effective fifth column work of the entire war was done in Hawaii, with the possible exception of Norway." Knox's assessment turned out to be inaccurate, for investigations by Naval Intelligence, Military Intelligence, and the Federal Bureau of Investigation all agreed that no sabotage had, in fact, occurred. But Knox's alarming announcement fueled rumors of Japanese subversive activities.[65]

Meanwhile, a confidential report on the question of Japanese-American loyalty had already been submitted to President Franklin Roosevelt. The president had secretly arranged to have Chicago businessman Curtis Munson gather intelligence on the Japanese in the United States and assess whether they constituted an internal military threat. In his discussion on sabotage and espionage, Munson informed the president that there was no need to fear America's Japanese population: "There will be no armed uprising of Japanese [in this country]. . . . Japan will commit some sabotage largely depending on imported Japanese as they are afraid of and do not trust the Nisei. There will be no wholehearted response from Japanese in the United States. . . . For the most part the local Japanese are loyal to the United States or, at worst, hope that by remaining quiet they can avoid concentration camps or irresponsible mobs. We do not believe that they would be at least any more disloyal than any other racial group in the United States with whom we went to war."[66]

The FBI conducted its own investigation of the Japanese. On December 10, Director J. Edgar Hoover informed the attorney general that "practically all" suspected individuals whom he had initially planned to arrest were in custody: 1,291 Japanese (367 in Hawaii, 924 on the mainland), 857 Germans, and 147 Italians. In a report to the attorney general submitted in early February, Hoover concluded that the proposed mass evacuation of the Japanese could not be justified for security reasons.[67]

Despite these intelligence findings, Lieutenant General John L. DeWitt, head of the Western Defense Command, requested approval to conduct search-and-seizure operations to prevent alien Japanese from making radio transmissions to Japanese ships. The Justice Department refused to issue search warrants without probable cause, and the FBI determined that the problem was only a perceived one. In January, the Federal Communications Commission, which had been monitoring all broadcasts, reported that the Army's fears were groundless. But the Army continued pursuing plans based on an assumption of Japanese disloyalty. General DeWitt also asked for the power to exclude Japanese aliens, as well as Americans of Japanese ancestry, from restricted areas. On January 4, 1942, at a meeting of federal and state officials in his Presidio headquarters, DeWitt argued that military necessity justified exclusion: "We are at war and this area — eight states — has been designated as a theater of operations. . . . [There are] approximately 288,000 enemy aliens . . . we have to watch. . . . I have little confidence that the enemy aliens are law-abiding or loyal in any sense of the word. Some of them yes; many, no. Particularly the Japanese. I have no confidence in their loyalty whatsoever. I am speaking now of the native born Japanese — 117,000 — and 42,000 in California alone."[68] Later, General DeWitt put it more bluntly: he told reporters in an off-the-record press conference that "a Jap is a Jap."[69]

FBI Director Hoover thought that the Western Defense Command's intelligence information reflected "hysteria and lack of judgment." The claim of military necessity for mass evacuation, he observed, was based "primarily upon public and political pressure rather than on factual data."[70]

Immediately after the press was told by Navy Secretary Knox about the alleged Japanese subversive activity at Pearl Harbor, West Coast newspapers gave the claim headline attention: "Fifth Column Treachery Told" and "Secretary of Navy Blames 5th Column for Raid." On January 5, John B. Hughes of the Mutual Broadcasting Company began firing a month-long salvo against the Japanese in California. The Japanese were engaged in espionage, he charged, and their dominance in produce production and control of the food supply were part of a master war plan.[71] On January 19, *Time* reported Japanese fifth-column activities in Hawaii, in an article entitled "The Stranger within Our Gates." The next day, the *San Diego Union* stirred anti-Japanese hysteria: "In Hawaii . . . treachery by residents, who although of Japanese ancestry had been regarded as loyal, has played an important part in the success of Japanese attacks. . . . Every Japanese . . . should be moved out of the coastal area and to a point of safety far enough inland to nullify any inclination they may have to tamper with our safety here."[72] The *Los Angeles Times* editorialized: "A viper is nonetheless a viper wherever the egg is hatched — so a Japanese American, born of Japanese parents — grows up to be a Japanese, not an American."[73]

As the press mounted its campaign for Japanese removal, it was joined by patriotic organizations. American Legion posts in Washington and Oregon passed resolutions urging the evacuation of all Japanese. In the January issue of their publication, *The Grizzly Bear,* the Native Sons and Daughters of the Golden West told their fellow Californians: "We told you so. Had the warnings been heeded — had the federal and state authorities been 'on the alert,' and rigidly enforced the Exclusion Law and the Alien Land Law . . . the treacherous Japs probably would not have attacked Pearl Harbor December 7, 1941, and this country would not today be at war with Japan."[74]

Beginning in January and early February, the anti-Japanese chorus included voices from farming interests, such as the Grower-Shipper Vegetable Association, the Western Growers Protective Association, and the California Farm Bureau Federation. "We've been charged with wanting to get rid of the Japs for selfish reasons," the Grower-Shipper Vegetable Association stated in the *Saturday Evening Post* in May. "We might as well be honest. We do. It's a question of whether the white man lives on the Pacific Coast or the brown man. They came into this valley to work, and they stayed to take over. . . . If all the Japs were removed tomorrow, we'd never miss them in two weeks, because the white farmers can take over and produce everything the Jap grows."[75]

Meanwhile, local and state politicians were already leading the movement for Japanese removal. California Attorney General Earl Warren pressed federal authorities to remove Japanese from sensitive areas on the West Coast. The Japanese in California, he warned, "may well be the Achilles['] heel of the entire civilian defense effort. Unless something is done it may bring about a repetition of Pearl Harbor."[76]

On February 1, in a telephone conversation with provost marshal General Allen Gullion, General DeWitt said he had "travelled up and down the West Coast," talked to "all the Governors and other local civil authorities," and decided to press for mass evacuation. Protection against sabotage, he argued, "only can be made positive by removing those people who are aliens and who are Japs of American citizenship." On February 5, after he received DeWitt's views in writing, Gullion drafted a War Department proposal for the exclusion of "all persons, whether aliens or citizens . . . deemed dangerous as potential saboteurs" from designated "military areas."[77]

During lunch with President Roosevelt on February 7, Attorney General Francis Biddle advised him that "there were no reasons for mass evacuation."[78] However, Roosevelt decided to approve General DeWitt's recommendation for the removal of Japanese Americans from the West Coast. DeWitt offered a justication: "In the war in which we are now engaged racial affinities are not severed by migration. The Japanese race is an enemy race and while many second and third generation Japanese born on United States soil, possessed of United States citizenship, have become 'Americanized,' the racial strains are undiluted. . . . It, therefore, follows that along the vital Pacific Coast over 112,000 potential enemies, of Japanese extraction, are at large today."[79]

On February 19, 1942, President Roosevelt signed Executive Order 9066, authorizing the evacuation and internment of Japanese Americans on the West Coast. And so it happened, tragically for the Japanese and for the U. S. Constitution, for there was actually no "military necessity."

Under General DeWitt's command, the military ordered a curfew for all enemy aliens and persons of Japanese ancestry and posted orders for evacuation. Years later, Congressman Robert Matsui, who was a baby in 1942, asked: "How could I as a 6-month-old child born in this country be declared by my own Government to be an enemy alien?"[80] Young Matsui and some 120,000 Japanese were removed: two-thirds of them were U.S. citizens by birth.

As they left their communities, the Japanese Americans felt the loss of everything familiar. One of them was the father of Norman Mineta, who, years later, would be elected to the U.S. House of Representatives. "I looked at Santa Clara's streets from the train over the subway," he wrote in a letter to friends in San Jose. "I thought this might be the last look at my loved home city. My heart almost broke, and suddenly hot tears just came pouring out. . . ."[81] They knew that more than their homes and possessions had been taken from them. "On May 16, 1942, my mother, two sisters, niece, nephew, and I left . . . by train," said Teru Watanabe. "Father joined us later. Brother left earlier by bus. We took whatever we could carry. So much we left behind, but the most valuable thing I lost was my freedom."[82]

Trains took the Japanese Americans to ten internment camps — Topaz in Utah, Poston and Gila River in Arizona, Amache in Colorado, Jerome and Rohwer in Arkansas, Minidoka in Idaho, Manzanar and Tule Lake in California, and Heart Mountain in Wyoming.

Years earlier, many of them had crossed the Pacific Ocean, sailing east to America. They had come here with extravagant hopes of settling in a new country. One of them captured the excitement in a poem:

> Day of spacious dreams!
> I sailed for America,
> Overblown with hope.[83]

Working hard, the immigrants had transformed the dusty valleys of California, these "wide wilderness fields into fertile land," "fresh green rows of strawberries reaching as far as the eye could see."[84] In their adopted land, they had created homes and communities. But now they found themselves imprisoned in internment camps. Looking around at the desolate landscape and barbed wire fences, some of the older ones were seized with melancholy:

> When the war is over
> And after we are gone
> Who will visit
> This lonely grave in the wild
> Where my friend lies buried?[85]

During World War II, over 30,000 Japanese Americans proved their loyalty by fighting bravely in the U.S. Army. Japanese-American soldiers of the 442nd Infantry Regiment suffered 9,486 casualties, including 600 killed. "Just think of all those people — of the 990 that went over [with me], not more than 200 of them came back without getting hit," said veteran Shig Doi. "If you look at the 442nd boys, don't look at their faces, look at their bodies. They got hit hard, some lost their limbs." The 442nd, military observers agreed, was probably the most decorated unit in United States military history. They earned 18,143 individual decorations — including 1 Congressional Medal of Honor, 47 Distinguished Service Crosses, 350 Silver Stars, 810 Bronze Stars, and more than 3,600 Purple Hearts.[86] One of these Japanese-American soldiers explained the meaning of their sacrifice in the war. In a letter to a friend, he wrote from the European battlefront during the war:

> My friends and my family — they mean everything to me. They are the most important reason why I am giving up my education and my happiness to go to fight a war that we never asked for. But our Country is involved in it. Not only that. By virtue of the Japanese attack on our nation, we as American citizens of Japanese ancestry have been mercilessly flogged with criticism and accusations. But I'm not going to take it sitting down! I may not be able to come back. But that matters little. My family and friends — they are the ones who will be able to back their arguments with facts. They are the ones who will be proud. In fact, it is better that we are sent to the front and that a few of us do not return, for the testimony will be stronger in favor of the folks back home.[87]

Into the Maelstrom of Race

Men and women make history, a philosopher once said, but they make it in circumstances they did not choose.[88] A long history of race in our nation provided a context for the lives and thoughts of Americans long before Japan's attack on Pearl Harbor. In the early twentieth century, deeply rooted stereotypes conditioned perceptions and attitudes of many individuals, including a future president.

As a young man, Harry Truman had harbored prejudices. In a letter to his future wife, Bess, he wrote on June 22, 1911: "Speaking of diamonds, would you wear a solitaire on your left hand should I get it? Now that is a rather personal or pointed question provided you take it for all it means." Nervous, the young suitor quickly changed the subject: "I think one man is as good as another so long as he's honest and decent and not a nigger or a Chinaman. Uncle Will [Young, the Confederate veteran] says that the Lord made a white man of dust, a nigger from mud, then threw up what was left and it came down a Chinaman. He does hate Chinese and Japs. So do I. It is race prejudice I guess. But I am strongly of the opinion that negroes ought to be in Africa, yellow men in Asia, and white men in Europe and America."[89]

As settlers on the Missouri frontier, the Trumans had encounters with Indians. In a letter to Bess, Truman described one incident: "Grandmother once routed a whole band of Indians with a big dog. She was all alone except for a negro woman and her two children. These Indians told her they wanted honey and if she didn't give it, they would take it and her too. So they sharpened their knives on the grinding stone and then she turned loose a large dog. Away went Indians, some leaving their blankets. If I had been Grandma I'd have disappeared out the front way when they came up the back. But she didn't and finally made them go."[90]

The Trumans had also been slaveholders. Asked, during an interview, about his grandparents and slavery, Truman said: "Oh, yes. They all had slaves. They brought them out here wit⌐

them from Kentucky. Most of the slaves were wedding presents." Truman was then asked whether it was a custom at the time to give slaves as wedding presents. "Yes, it was quite common. When a young couple got married, they got a few slaves to start out housekeeping with." An average white family would have five or six slaves. "They'd have a cook and a nurse for the children and a maid-of-all-work. Then maybe they'd have a couple of field hands to a go along with them."[91]

When the Civil War came, Truman's mother supported the Confederacy. According to Merle Miller, who interviewed retired President Truman, she thought it was "a good thing when Lincoln was shot." Truman recalled an incident: "When my mother and sister came to Washington at the time I was . . . in the White House, my brother had told my mother that the one bed that was not occupied was the one in the Lincoln Room, and she said, 'You tell Harry if he tries to put me in Lincoln's bed, I'll sleep on the floor,' and she would have."[92]

Independence, Missouri, was a segregated town. Blacks lived in a neighborhood called "Nigger Neck." The Trumans had black servants. Truman cherished his childhood memories of blacks, especially those of a "good old black woman" who had worked for his family as a cook and washerwoman. "All of us called her Auntie. We were all as fond of her as we were of our kinfolks. . . . When Auntie died, we all felt as if we'd lost a member of the family."[93] In a letter to Bess, August 4, 1939, Truman described accompanying Auntie to the park: "Well, this is nigger picnic day. But they don't have 'em like they did in days past. I remember once going to Washington Park with our washerwoman to a Fourth of August celebration. I'll never forget it. Had chicken and catfish fried in corn meal and was it good!"[94]

Families like the Trumans, biographer David McCullough noted, usually used words like "nigger" and "coon."[95] Such terms may not have been intentionally derogatory, but they were freighted with notions of black inferiority stemming from a history of slavery. The infusion of racial epithets in daily communication gave them added power, making such language seem normal. Truman was part of this culture. While courting Bess, the young Truman had written to her: "That is one reason I like being a farmer. Even if you do have to work like a coon you know that you are not grinding the life out of someone else to live yourself."[96] On another occasion, he complained: "I was assistant wash lady yesterday. You ought to see me in that role. Since our nigger woman busted a beer bottle over her old man's head and ran away, we have had to do our own washing."[97] In a letter dated March 23, 1912, Truman described John Greenleaf Whittier as "the old nigger lover."[98]

After Truman entered politics, he continued to make the same racial references. In a letter to Bess dated August 9, 1930, from Duluth, Minnesota, Truman commented on the residents: "They're all from the Scandinavian peninsula or Denmark or Finland, all blonds and most of 'em talk with an accent. I've only seen one nigger and he was bleached out to a pale yellow."[99] While looking for an apartment in Washington, D.C., he wrote to Bess on July 17, 1935: "There was one at 1726 Massachusetts that's a dandy but the rent's too much. It had a grand hall, living room and dining room, two bedrooms, two baths, and closets galore, two-car garage and a Missouri nigger for a janitor — graduate of Lincoln University at Jefferson City."[100] On January 6, 1936, Truman joked in a letter to Bess: "He and I and old Senator Coolidge and Barkley were the only ones not dressed, as Jimmy Byrnes [the future secretary of state] said, like nigga preachers."[101] In a letter to Bess on September 15, 1940, Truman jokingly described how he was writing "as impudently as a sassy nigger."[102]

Even after the Civil Rights movement was underway, Tru-

The "Day of Infamy," Pearl Harbor, December 7, 1941.

Truman and Roosevelt, August 18, 1944.
Breakfast at the White House after the
1944 Democratic National Convention.

Truman sworn in as president, April 12,
1944.

The Bataan Death
March: American
prisoners of war.

A propaganda postcard
of World War II.

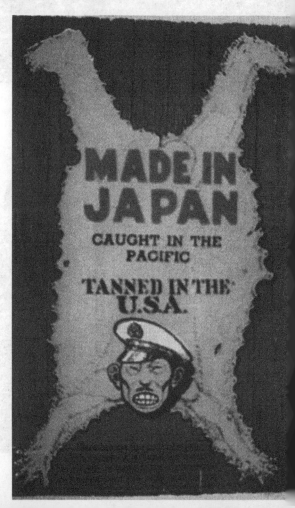

Secretary of War Henry L. Stimson and aide, Colonel William H. Kyle, at Potsdam, July 15, 1945.

President Truman, Secretary of State James Byrnes, and Admiral William Leahy at the Potsdam Conference, July 16, 1945.

The Alamogordo explosion — a midday sun.

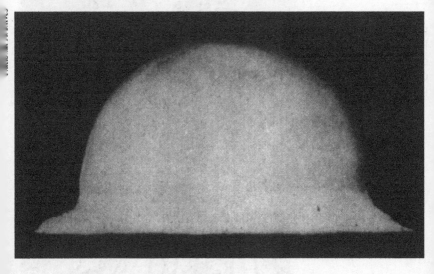

Winston Churchill,
Harry Truman, and
Joseph Stalin at the
Potsdam Conference,
July 24, 1945.

Dr. J. Robert Oppen-
heimer and Major
General Leslie R.
Groves at the site of the
first atomic explosion.

The final day of the Potsdam Conference, August 1, 1945.
Prime Minister Clement Attlee, President Truman, and
Premier Stalin. *Second row*: Admiral Leahy, Foreign
Minister Ernest Bevin, Secretary of State Byrnes, and
Foreign Commissar V. Molotov.

The *Enola Gay*.

"Little Boy," replica of the atomic bomb dropped on Hiroshima.

"Fat Man," replica of the atomic bomb dropped on Nagasaki, August 9, 1945.

The atomic mushroom cloud over Hiroshima, August 6, 1945.

President Truman with the 100/442 Regimental Combat Team of Japanese-American soldiers, at the White House.

Truman announces the
surrender of Japan,
August 14, 1945.

Truman selected "Man
of the Year," *Time,*
December 31, 1945.

man continued to use these racial terms. While being interviewed by Miller in 1961–2, Truman described something that had happened when he escorted Franklin Roosevelt's casket to the White House on April 14: "We went up to Union Station to meet the body, and when we started back to the White House, the streets were just jammed. People on both sides of the streets when we brought the body back, people were crowded together, and people were crying. I saw one old nigger woman sitting down on the curb with her apron up to her eyes just crying her eyes out." During one of the interviews, Truman also complained about how visitors to Independence would not leave him alone: "There are always curiosity seekers waiting out there, and you sometimes can't even go out to get the papers. You have to send the old nigger cook out to do it for you." Commenting on the retired president's way of referring to blacks, Miller noted: "Privately Mr. Truman always said 'nigger'; at least he always did when I talked to him." Miller connected Truman's racial vocabulary to the fact that the former president was from a "Southern" town, where one of the prominent organizations was the United Daughters of the Confederacy.[103]

Truman opposed social equality for blacks. On July 14, 1940, he told the National Colored Democratic Association in Chicago: "I wish to make it clear that I am not appealing for social equality for the Negro. The Negro himself knows better than that, and the highest type of Negro leaders say quite frankly that they prefer the society of their own people. Negroes want justice, not social relations." In 1944, as the vice-presidential candidate, Truman was quoted as saying that if blacks sat at a counter in a drugstore in Independence, "they would be booted out" because the management of such stores had a right to refuse to serve them.[104]

However, Truman's views on race were actually complex. He supported anti-lynching and anti–poll tax legislation. In 1940,

Truman spoke out against the Klan: "I believe in the brother-hood of man, not merely the brotherhood of white men but the brotherhood of all men before the law. I believe in the Constitution and the Declaration of Independence. In giving Negroes the rights which are theirs we are only acting in accord with our own ideals of a true democracy. The majority of our Negro people find cold comfort in shanties and tenements. Surely, as freemen, they are entitled to something better than this. . . . It is our duty to see that Negroes in our locality have increased opportunity to exercise their privilege as freemen. . . ."[105]

Later, after World War II, President Truman desegregated the armed forces, mandating the end of racially separate facilities and training programs. He also issued an executive order for a policy of "fair employment throughout the Federal establishment, without discrimination because of race, color, religion or national origin."[106] In fact, Truman acquired an impressive civil rights record. "I had tremendous opposition from the South," he recalled after he retired, "with the racial sections of my Fair Deal program, in which, among other things, I proposed the end to the poll tax [and] the retention of the Fair Employment Practices Committee so that black people could continue to be protected and get their share of jobs."[107]

Truman said he believed that everybody should be treated fairly and was entitled to equality before the law. In one of his historical essays, he criticized President Theodore Roosevelt for extending the 1882 Chinese Exclusion Act. "I wasn't old enough to pay much attention to it, but a lot of people in California and the rest of the West Coast thought it was a good thing. They said they didn't want cheap labor competing with Americans in California or Oregon or Washington. The cry was, how can a man who has to have two dollars a day compete with a man who can live on two cents a day?" Such thinking, Truman argued, was "nonsense, because immigrants learn very quickly

about the joys of living better." In his view, the Chinese de-
served the same treatment as American laborers.[108]

During World War II, Truman opposed the internment of
Japanese Americans. When he was asked by interviewer Merle
Miller to comment on Japanese-American relocation, the retired
president replied: "They were concentration camps. They called
it relocation, but they put them in concentration camps, and I
was against it. We were in a period of emergency, but it was
still the wrong thing to do. It was one place where I never went
along with Roosevelt. He never should have allowed it." Referring to the fact that Americans of German and Italian descent
had not been interned, Miller asked: "Do you suppose it was
because Americans of Japanese descent looked different?" Truman replied: "It may have been. But the reason it happened was
just the same as what we've been talking about [hysteria].
People out on the West Coast got scared, and they panicked,
and they decided to get rid of the Japanese-Americans."[109]

Although he was critical of wartime hysteria as it related to
Japanese-American internment, Truman was also swept into the
anti-Japanese maelstrom of race hate and revenge. He, too, was
bitter and angry at the Japanese for their surprise attack on Pearl
Harbor, their atrocities, such as the Bataan death march, and
their murderous defense of islands like Luzon and Okinawa.
Rejecting Churchill's suggestion for a revision of the unconditional surrender demand that would have allowed Japan to end
the war with honor, Truman stated that the Japanese did not
have any honor after their dastardly attack.[110]

The dropping of the atomic bomb, without warning, would
be America's surprise attack. In his diary at Potsdam on July
22, 1945, Truman kept thinking about Pearl Harbor as he prepared his order to drop the atomic bomb on Japan: "Raised a
flag over our area in Berlin. It is the flag raised in Rome, North
Africa and Paris. Flag was over the White House when Pearl

Harbor happened. Will be raised over Tokyo." In his diary entries written during his tense negotiations with Stalin, Truman frequently flayed the "Japs." He recorded in his diary that Stalin had agreed to enter the war against Japan: "He'll be in the Jap War on August 15th. Fini Japs when that comes about." Informed about the explosion at Alamogordo, Truman scribbled in his diary: "Discussed Manhattan (it is a success). Decided to tell Stalin about it. Stalin had told P.M. [Churchill] of telegram from Jap emperor asking for peace. Stalin also read his answer to me. It was satisfactory. Believe Japs will fold up before Russia comes in. I am sure they will when Manhattan appears over their homeland." Prepared to unleash terrible destruction, Truman described in his diary the enemy as the "Japs" — "savages, ruthless, merciless and fanatic."[111]

After the bombing of Hiroshima, Truman remembered Pearl Harbor: "The Japanese began the war from the air at Pearl Harbor. They have been repaid manyfold."[112] In a private letter, Truman justified the bombing: "Nobody is more disturbed over the unwarranted attack by the Japanese on Pearl Harbor and their murder of our prisoners of war. The only language they seem to understand is the one that we have been using to bombard them. When you have to deal with a beast you have to treat him as a beast. It is most regrettable but true."[113]

In this "war without mercy," Truman made the deadly mushroom cloud of "Manhattan" appear over Japan in order to destroy an enemy he regarded as "a beast."[114]

6

WHERE THE BUCK STOPPED

> The timid man, the lazy man, the man who distrusts his country, the overcivilized man, who has lost the great fighting, masterful virtues, the ignorant man, the man of dull mind, whose soul is incapable of feeling the mighty lift that thrills "stern men with empires in their brains" — all these, of course, shrink from seeing the nation undertake its new duties; shrink from seeing us build a navy and an army adequate to our needs; shrink from seeing us do our share of the world's work, by bringing order out of chaos. . . .
>
> Theodore Roosevelt,
> "The Strenuous Life"[1]

An "Accidental" President

"I tried never to forget who I was and where I'd come from and where I was going back to," Harry Truman said after he retired from the presidency.[2] But his past was not a source of self-esteem. As a child, he was regarded as average, not someone with a promising future, and certainly not a future president.

"When Harry was in school, well, we all liked Harry," retired schoolteacher Miss Zuba Chiles recalled, "and he always got his lessons but never beyond that. . . . Nobody thought that he'd go far at all." The retired president confirmed her memory: "Nobody ever thought I was going to amount to much, and that's why when people are always asking about the records of when I was a boy and so on, the answer is nobody kept any records because nobody thought it was necessary."[3]

Truman always considered himself as "just an old Missouri farmer." His mother-in-law, Madge Gates Wallace, was from a wealthy family — "topnotchers" and "high society" in Missouri. She lived with her daughter and Truman from the time of their marriage until her death in 1952. He was not what Mrs. Wallace had in mind as a son-in-law, and she never fully reconciled herself to the union. The Trumans were "dirt farmers," Mrs. Wallace said frequently, even in her son-in-law's presence.[4]

Perhaps that was the reason Bess had initially rejected his marriage proposal. "You know that you turned me down so easy that I am almost happy anyway," Truman wrote to Bess on July 12, 1911. "I was never fool enough to think that a girl like you could ever care for a fellow like me but I couldn't help telling you how I felt. I have always wanted you to have some fine, rich, good-looking man."[5]

Truman persisted, and eventually he succeeded in winning her hand. After many years of marriage, he recalled in a letter to Bess: "Thirty years ago I hoped to make you a happy wife and a happy mother. Did I? I don't know. All I can say [is] I've tried. There is no one in the world anyway who can look down on you or your daughter. That means much to me, but I've never cared for social position or rank for myself except to see that those dear to me were not made to suffer for my shortcomings."[6]

Truman was very aware of his "shortcomings." He did not have a college education. He had hoped to receive a free education at West Point. "But because of my eyes, I didn't get to go, of course." Instead of college, he went to work. "I was eighteen years old, and I'd just finished high school and knew I wasn't going to get to go to West Point," Truman recalled. "So I took this job as a timekeeper. I took it to help out at home, to keep my brother, Vivian, and my sister, Mary, in school. My father was having a hard time with finances just then."[7]

Truman served in the army during World War I and then operated a clothing store that went bankrupt. "My God, at forty he hadn't succeeded at anything," reporter Merle Miller noted, "and he had a wife and a baby and an insupportable mother-in-law to support." A failure in business, Truman entered politics to earn a livelihood. He was elected to a judgeship with the help of the Pendergast machine. Asked how he happened to get into politics, Truman replied: "In 1922 I had gone broke trying to run a haberdashery store, and I had to have a job. And I had a lot of good friends in Jackson County and was kin to everybody else, and so I ran for eastern judge, one of five, and I licked all the rest of them because I knew more people in the county than they did."[8]

Truman had not wanted to become the vice-presidential nominee. One of his friends recalled saying to him: "Harry, whoever gets that Vice Presidential nomination is going to be President because there is no man alive who can be in that job for sixteen years." And Truman replied: "I know. I know, and that is why I do not want the nomination." Then he added: "Responsibility is just too great."[9]

But Truman happened to become the vice-presidential candidate with Roosevelt. At the Chicago convention in 1944, the Democratic party was split between the liberal Henry Wallace and the conservative James Byrnes for the nomination. Truman was preparing to nominate Byrnes; suddenly he was told that he had been selected as Roosevelt's running mate. He received the surprising news while eating a hot dog with mustard.[10]

This choice for vice president aroused concern, however. Everyone was aware of the fact that Roosevelt was ill and that he might not be able to complete his next term. Roosevelt had chosen "a little machine politician," a reporter commented. "But if anything should happen to President Roosevelt during his fourth term, I fear the direst consequences. We shall have as our leader a political hack when we could have had a great man."[11]

Truman, too, worried that something might happen to the great leader. "Oh, yes, I was scared," Truman told an interviewer after he retired. He was anxious "all the time" about the possibility that he would suddenly be forced to become the nation's helmsman. "It was a terrible thing to have to take over after a three-term President who had been so nearly unanimously elected every time," Truman recalled. "It was something to worry about, and I did worry about it."[12] Then Truman's "worst" nightmare happened.[13]

On April 12, the new president recorded his apprehensions in his diary: "I was very much shocked. I am not easily shocked but was certainly shocked when I was told of the President's death and the weight of the Government had fallen on my shoulders."[14] In a letter to his mother written that night, the nervous son confided: "It was the only time in my life, I think, that I ever felt as if I'd had a real shock."[15]

Truman had become president, to use his own words, "more or less by accident."[16]

Years later, in his *Memoirs*, Truman admitted that he had been "unprepared" to assume the presidency.[17] As vice president, he had found himself isolated and kept uninformed about foreign policy. "The truth is Roosevelt knew very little about Mr. Truman," reporter Miller noted. "The Trumans hadn't even been invited to the White House to break bread with the Roosevelts. . . ."[18] More important, Truman had been left out of Roosevelt's policymaking circles. He had attended only two scheduled meetings with Roosevelt. According to his daughter, Margaret, Vice President Truman referred to himself as "a political eunuch."[19] He had been given very little responsibility. In his diary on April 11, Truman described the boredom of his functionless office: "I have to work and I'm trying to make a job out of the Vice Presidency and it's quite a chore."[20]

The very next day, Truman suddenly became president and was burdened with a multitude of seemingly overwhelming chores. Most worrisome was the responsibility of handling international relations. Truman told his first postmaster general, Frank Walker: "I know nothing of foreign affairs, and I must acquaint myself with them at once."[21] In his diary on April 12, he admitted his ignorance in these matters: "I knew the President had a great many meetings with Churchill and Stalin. I was not familiar with any of these things and it was really something to think about but I decided the best thing was to go home and get as much rest as possible and face the music."[22] Little wonder the new president was insecure. "Overwhelming responsibilities" had suddenly crashed on him.[23] "I was plenty scared, but, of course, I didn't let anybody see it," Truman recalled years later.[24]

Shortly after he had been sworn in as president, however, Truman found himself unable to conceal his trepidation. "Boys, if you ever pray, pray for me now," Truman told reporters. "I don't know whether you fellows ever had a load of hay fall on you, but when they told me . . . what had happened, I felt like the moon, the stars, and all the planets had fallen on me."[25] He felt like he had been struck by "lightning."[26] He confided to his friend, Senator George D. Aiken of Vermont: "I'm not big enough. I'm not big enough for this job."[27]

What made his job especially difficult was the sting of personal indignities and sarcasms. Roosevelt's death prompted snide remarks: "Good God, Truman will be President." "If Truman can be President, so could my next-door neighbor."[28] *Time* described the new president as "a man of distinct limitations, especially in experience in high level politics."[29] The *New York Times* characterized Roosevelt's successor as "a cardboard figure."[30]

Reporter Miller vividly recalled the death of Roosevelt: "I was in Paris in the shabby office on the rue de Berri, where the European edition of *Yank* was, always haphazardly, put together. We were playing poker, with the radio turnd low. Suddenly the music — was it 'Don't Sit Under the Apple Tree'? — was interrupted, and the sorrowing voice of a sergeant on the Armed Forces Network said, 'President Franklin D. Roosevelt died this afternoon at. . . .'" Like millions of others, Miller remarked: "My God, now we're left with Harry Truman. Are we in trouble?" Miller bluntly pointed out "one of the biggest things wrong with Harry Truman" — "he wasn't Franklin Roosevelt." Roosevelt was "imperial," but Truman looked and acted and talked like a "failed haberdasher."[31]

"One thing that especially worried my father," recalled his daughter, Margaret, "was the image of him as a bumbling, ineffectual second-rater that many newspapers had striven to construct during the campaign." She also reported that Truman "snorted with indignation when someone called him 'the little man in the White House.'"[32] This characterization, Truman himself admitted, did "bother me a bit."[33]

But what distressed Truman more profoundly was the immense challenge he faced as the successor to a great president. In his diary on the night of April 12, Truman wrote: "I did not know what reaction the country would have to the death of a man whom they all practically worshipped."[34]

The reactions included not only grief for the president who was gone, but also doubt about the president who now was in Roosevelt's shoes. On April 12, Secretary of War Stimson wrote in his diary that Truman "knew very little of the task into which he was stepping and he showed some vacillation on minor matters that came up for decision a little bit as if he might be lacking in force." The next day, Stimson continued to contrast the two presidents. "Roosevelt had such immense prestige politically arising from his four successful campaigns for President," wrote Stimson in his diary, "that he carried a weight with the Congress and with general politicians in the country which Truman could not possibly have."[35] In the loved and respected Roosevelt, Americans had come to place their hopes for peace.

When chief of staff Admiral William D. Leahy learned about Roosevelt's death, he felt the immensity of the loss. In his memoir, he recalled: "This tragedy deprived the nation of its individual, irreplaceable leader at a time when the war to preserve civilization was approaching its end with accelerated speed. Franklin Roosevelt was a world figure of heroic proportions." Then Leahy expressed deep doubts: "One could hardly see at the time how the complicated, critical business of the war and peace could be carried forward by a new President who was, in comparison, almost completely inexperienced in international affairs."[36] Earlier, when Truman had been nominated for the vice presidency, Leahy had exclaimed: "Who the hell is Harry Truman?"[37]

Three days after Roosevelt's death, in the mountains of Los Alamos, the director of the weapons laboratory, J. Robert Oppenheimer, gave a short speech to the atomic scientists gathered for a memorial service. He said that when word of the president's death arrived, many who were "unaccustomed to tears, many men and women, little enough accustomed to prayer, prayed to God. Many of us looked with deep trouble to the future; many of us felt less certain that our works would be to a good end. . . ." Oppenheimer then reflected on how Americans had lost a leader during a time of stress and fear. "We have been living through years of great evil, and of great terror. Roosevelt has been our President, Our Commander-in-

Chief. . . . All over the world men have looked to him for guidance, and have seen symbolized in him their hope that the evils of this time would not be repeated. . . ."[38]

Oppenheimer and Americans everywhere now had to transfer their hope and trust to the new president. Unsure of himself and worried about his inexperience, Truman was determined to show the world that the "plain" Truman could replace the "patrician" Roosevelt. He would show those stuffed-shirt lawyers with their "Ha-vud accents" where to get off. He would tell them: "If you can't stand the heat, stay out of the kitchen." He would honor the quote from Mark Twain that he kept on on his desk in the White House: "Always do right. This will gratify some people & astonish the rest."[39]

Insecure but armed with determination, Truman raised his right hand, took the oath of office, and became president on April 12. He realized he had to demonstrate decisiveness in order to command the respect of the policymakers around him. He quickly impressed the secretary of war. Remembering how Roosevelt had encouraged the play of differing ideas in making policy, Stimson noticed that Truman preferred making rapid judgments. In his diary on April 18, Stimson welcomed working with this new style: "It was a wonderful relief to preceding conferences with our former Chief to see the promptness and snappiness with which Truman took up each matter and decided it." The new president also won the admiration of the acting secretary of state. "When I saw him today," wrote Joseph Grew only a month after Truman took office, "I had fourteen problems to take up with him and got through them in less than fifteen minutes with a clear directive on every one of them. You can imagine what a joy it is to deal with a man like that."[40]

Similarly, to the ambassador to Russia, Truman showed his ability to take command quickly and firmly. "I had talked with Mr. Truman for only a few minutes," reported W. Averell

Harriman, "when I began to realize that the man had a real grasp of the situation. What a surprise and relief this was! . . . I want[ed] . . . Molotov . . . to learn from the very highest source that we would not stand for any pushing around on the Polish question. And I hoped the President would back me up. When I left that first conference with him that day, I knew the President's mind didn't need any making up from me on that point."[41]

While Truman stated that he intended to continue Roosevelt's foreign and domestic policies, he was determined that he would be president in his own right and that he would assume "full responsibility for such decisions as had to be made."[42] He would be a president who could "make up his own mind." "All final decisions," he firmly declared, "would be mine."[43]

One of them would change the entire course of world history and also help define Truman as a decisive president.

The Diplomacy of Masculinity

Ironically, when he was a child, this strong president had been regarded as effeminate and weak. At the age of six, Truman developed problems with his eyes. His mother noticed that he had "flat eye-balls." His doctor prescribed glasses. "I was so carefully cautioned by the eye doctor about breaking my glasses and injuring my eyes that I was afraid to join in the rough-and-tumble games in the schoolyard and the back lot." Truman was nearly blind without his glasses.[44]

The boys in the neighborhood called him "*four-eyes* and a lot of other things, too." Henry Chiles, a childhood neighbor, remembered how the boys "used to call Harry a sissy. He wore glasses and didn't play our games. He carried books, and we'd carry a baseball bat. So we called him a sissy." Years later, as president, Truman was asked by a youngster: "Mr. President, was you popular when you was a little boy?" Truman answered: "Why, no, I was never popular. The popular boys were the ones who were good at games and [had] big, tight fists. I was never like that. Without my glasses I was blind as a bat, and to tell the truth, I was a kind of sissy. If there was any danger of getting into a fight, I always ran."[45]

Recalling his identity as a "sissy," the retired president Truman admitted: "That's hard on a boy. It makes him lonely, and it gives him an inferiority complex, and he has a hard time overcoming it."[46]

Young Truman retreated into the world of books. "I always had my nose stuck in a book, a history book mostly. . . . There were about three thousand books in the library downtown, and I guess I read them all, including the encyclopedias."[47] Stories of great men especially interested him, and a volume entitled *Soldiers and Sailors* seized his imagination. He dreamed of growing up to become a great general.[48]

But the library and his fantasies did not protect the insecure boy from the teasing of his friends or family. In a letter to Bess on April 8, 1912, Truman described an incident: "My dear brother had to go and get his shoulder dislocated when I started the [letter], and I was shaken up so on hearing it I couldn't write. That sounds rather feminine, doesn't it? Mamma says I was intended for a girl anyway. It makes me pretty mad to be told so but I guess it's partly so."[49]

Regarded as feminine, Truman felt special pressure from his family to be manly. He was named after his Uncle Harrison Young. During the Civil War, Federal troops had raided the Young home; Solomon Young, Harrison's father, was away at the time. "They tried to make my Uncle Harrison into an informer, but he wouldn't do it," Truman told an interviewer. "He was only a boy, but he wouldn't turn informer. They tried to hang him, time and again they tried it, 'stretching his neck,' they called it, but he didn't say anything. I think he'd have died before he'd of said anything. He's the one I'm named after, and I'm happy to say that there were . . . people around at the time who said I took after him."[50] The nephew felt he had to live up to his namesake — Harrison.

Young Truman also had his father to emulate. John Anderson Truman was "a small, feisty man." "Everybody called him Peanuts."[51] But, recalled the retired president, he was "a fighter." "If he didn't like what you did, he'd fight you. He was an Andrew Jackson descendant, you understand, and those people are all fighters. He was five foot six and weighed a hundred and forty pounds, and he'd whip anybody up to two hundred if they got in his way."[52] Truman fondly remembered his father's "pugnacity." "No one ever pushed John Anderson Truman's children around without getting some sharp pushing in return," the president's daughter, Margaret, recalled. "My grandfather was very Southern in his hot-blooded instinct to defend his family at all costs. Dad never forgot the warm feeling his father's fights on his behalf aroused in him."[53]

Truman admired his father as a "determined cuss": "One day, when he was road supervisor, there was a big boulder across the road, and he lifted it off all by himself. He wouldn't let his crew help him. That's the kind of man he was. Well, it hurt him, and when we finally got him to go to the doctor . . . the hospital, it was too late. I was with him when he died. I dozed off, and when I woke up, he was gone. I'll never forget him, though. He was quite a man." Hearing this story, interviewer Miller asked the retired president: "Didn't you succeed your father as overseer of the roads?" "I did," he answered. Then Truman was asked whether he regarded his father as a success. "He was the father of a President of the United States, and I should think that that is success enough for any man."[54]

Called a "sissy," young Truman was determined to overcome

his "inferiority complex." He told himself: "You've got to fight for everything you do." During World War I, he became the commanding officer of Battery D; in charge of many soldiers, he wore his masculinity on his sleeve. "Now, look," he told his men, "I didn't come here to get along with you guys. You're going to have to get along with me, and if any of you thinks he can't, why, speak right up, and I'll give you a punch in the nose."[55]

Truman liked to display his toughness. Once he was irritated by an article by Paul Hume criticizing his daughter's musical ability. In an angry note, the father threatened to punch the journalist in the nose ("you'll need a new nose") and also to "kick his balls in."[56] "No one," Margaret boasted, "pushed Harry Truman around."[57]

Truman carried his bravado into politics. In 1940, he fought hard to win reelection to the Senate. "There were too many people around who didn't want me to run. I knew it was going to be a hell of a fight, but I've never backed away from a fight." During an interview after he retired, Truman was asked whether he had ever thought about becoming a concert pianist. Truman explained why he had given up studying music: "Because I decided that playing the piano wasn't the thing for a man to do. It was a sissy thing to do. So I just stopped. And it was probably all for the best. I wouldn't ever have been first-rate. A good music-hall piano player is about the best I'd have ever been. So I went into politics and became President of the United States."[58]

Determined not to do a "sissy thing," Truman turned to past leaders for lessons and inspiration: "I learned that in those periods of history when there was no leadership, society usually groped through dark ages of one degree or another. I saw that it takes men to make history."[59] A president should be strong: "There's always a lot of talk about how we have to fear the man on horseback, have to be afraid of the strong man, but so far,

if I have read my American history right, it isn't the strong men
that have caused us most of the trouble, it's the ones who were
weak. It's the ones who just sat on their asses and twiddled their
thumbs when they were President."[60]

As president, Truman would practice masculine diplomacy:
he would be a "man on horseback" when dealing with the Russians. During his first meeting with Soviet Foreign Minister
Vyacheslav M. Molotov, Truman ordered him to carry out the
agreements regarding Poland. Molotov protested: "I have never
been talked to like that in my life." Truman barked back: "Carry
out your agreements and you won't get talked to like that."[61]
Before leaving for the anticipated confrontation with Stalin at
Potsdam, Truman remarked: "We've got to teach them [the Rus-
sians] how to behave."[62]

At Potsdam, Truman resentfully felt that Stalin was pushing
him around. He thought the Russian leader was "an S.O.B.,"[63]
and he particularly did not like Stalin thinking of himself as
the "Big I Am."[64] When Truman first saw Stalin on July 17, he
sized him up: "I was surprised at Stalin's stature — he was not
over five feet five or six inches tall. When we had pictures taken,
he would usually stand on the step above me."[65] Called the
"little man," Truman was conscious of his own height; at five
feet eight, he seemed pleased to find that Stalin was shorter than
he.[66]

Moreover, Truman had a secret, and, in time, he would show
Stalin how "big" he, Truman, was. In his diary, he described
his first showdown with Stalin. The Russian leader had some
questions, so Truman told him to "fire away." "He did," Truman
wrote in his diary, "and it is dynamite — but I have some dynamite too which I'm not exploding now."[67]

The next day Truman learned about the first atomic explosion — his "dynamite" turned out to be 20,000 tons of TNT!
"The atomic bomb and its implications," Admiral William

Leahy recalled, "had been on the minds of all of us since we received at Potsdam . . . the news of the successful testing of the new weapon. From that date on, it was no longer a theory. We had the bombs."[68] As historian Martin Sherwin pointed out, the news from Alamogordo thrilled Truman. "The President was tremendously pepped up by it," Stimson reported in his diary. Truman said "it gave him an entirely new feeling of confidence."[69]

Winston Churchill also noticed the change in Truman's demeanor. "Fortified" by the exciting news of the bomb, the president "stood up to the Russians in a most emphatic and decisive manner."[70] Truman told the Soviets what demands "they absolutely could not have," and he "generally bossed the whole meeting."[71]

In a letter to Bess from Potsdam, July 20, 1945, Truman boasted: "We had a tough meeting yesterday. I reared up on my hind legs and told 'em where to get off and they got off. I have to make it perfectly plain to them at least once a day that so far as this President is concerned Santa Claus is dead and that my first interest is U.S.A., then I want the Jap War won and I want 'em both in it. But certainly am not going to set up another [illegible] here in Europe, pay reparations, feed the world, and get nothing for it but a nose thumbing. They are beginning to awake to the fact that I mean business."[72] Five days later, he wrote again: "Russia and Poland have gobbled up a big hunk of Germany and want Britain and us to agree. I have flatly refused. We have unalterably opposed the recognition of police governments in the German Axis countries. I told Stalin that until we had free access to those countries there'd never be recognition. He seems to like it when I hit him with a hammer."[73]

In many different ways, the language and notions of masculinity seemed to frame the way Truman and his policymakers viewed Russian expansionism and also the atomic bomb. They thought of international negotiations in terms of what it meant to act like men. They were not necessarily aware of these attitudes. Rather, they had grown up and were living in a culture that defined how men and women should behave. Shared with other societies but shaped by a uniquely American experience, these ideas of masculinity were so pervasive that they had become a natural way for Truman and the men around him to make policy.

Little wonder that the atomic bomb symbolized virility. The very success of the explosion at Alamogordo was described in a top secret message to Truman at Potsdam in terms of a father receiving news about the birth of his son:

> TO SECRETARY OF WAR FROM HARRISON. DOCTOR HAS JUST
> RETURNED MOST ENTHUSIASTIC AND CONFIDENT THAT THE
> LITTLE BOY IS AS HUSKY AS HIS BIG BROTHER. THE LIGHT IN
> HIS EYES DISCERNIBLE FROM HERE TO HIGHHOLD AND I
> COULD HAVE HEARD HIS SCREAMS HERE TO MY FARM.[74]

"Big Brother" was the bomb exploded in New Mexico, and "Little Boy" was the second bomb, ready for deployment against Japan. "Highhold" was Stimson's estate, 250 miles from Washington. "My farm" referred to George Harrison's [Interim Committee member] farm, located at Upperville, Virginia, forty miles from Washington. "The medical terminology baffled the young officers who were manning the American communications center at Potsdam," Margaret Truman commented. "They thought that seventy-seven-year-old Mr. Stimson had just become a father."[75]

Pugilistic terms also became metaphors for power diplomacy backed with atomic bombs. "In war, as in a boxing match," Stimson wrote, "it is seldom sound for the stronger combatant to moderate his blows whenever his opponent shows signs of weakening."[76] Boxing illustrated Truman's dramatic confrontation with Molotov. "I gave it to him straight," the president bragged. "I let him have it. It was the straight one-two to the jaw."[77] He wrote in his memoirs that he had decided to "lay it on the line with Molotov."[78] He saw Stalin as "tough mentally and physically," but, he wrote in his diary, "I can deal with Stalin."[79] The president talked about "ganging up" on the Soviet leader and Molotov.[80]

Similarly, Secretary of State Byrnes approached negotiating with the Russians as a competition, challenge, showdown, shootout, and fistfight. "We should not start something," Byrnes stated firmly, "we are not prepared to finish."[81] He was always sizing up the Soviet Union to see whether or not he would be able to "scare" his opponent with the bomb. "The only way to negotiate with the Russians is to hit them hard, and then negotiate," Byrnes argued.[82] Secretary of War Stimson also approached Russia as a pugilist. "It may be necessary," he wrote in his diary on May 15, "to have it out with Russia on her relations to Manchuria and Port Arthur and various other parts of North China, and also the relations of China to us."[83]

For these men, ball games became a reference point for what Theodore Roosevelt would have termed "strenuous" diplomacy.[84] The U.S. needed, Stimson thought, to "find some way of persuading Russia to play ball."[85] Truman instructed Harry Hopkins to be direct in his negotiations with Stalin: "I told Harry he could use diplomatic language, or he could use a baseball bat if he thought that was the proper approach to Mr. Stalin."[86] Even the complex bureaucracy of the Manhattan Project was explained in terms of male sports. General Groves described the concept of the Project's compartmentalization. "Just as outfielders should not think about the manager's job of changing the pitchers, and a blocker should not be worrying about the ball-carrier fumbling," he said of his staff, "each scientist had to be made to do his own work."[87]

Many of the policymakers enjoyed drinking and playing poker during what they called "bull bat time."[88] Averell Harriman recalled that at Potsdam, "Jimmy Byrnes played his cards pretty close to his vest."[89] Stimson described the strategy against Japan and also the stressful negotiations with Stalin in terms of a card game. "We held two cards to assist us in such an effort [to persuade Japan to surrender before an invasion]." One was the traditional veneration that the Japanese people held for their emperor and, consequently, his power over his loyal troops. "The second card was the use of the atomic bomb" in the manner best calculated to pressure the emperor to declare a surrender.[90]

But Japan was not the only player in this international poker game. Russia was at the table, too. In his diary on May 14, Stimson described the strategy against this opponent. The U.S. had two powerful cards to play against the Russians — economic leverage and the atomic bomb. Together, they were "a royal straight flush and we mustn't be a fool about the way we play it." Which cards one held would dictate the outcome of the game. The United States had cards that the Russians did not. "They [the Soviets] can't get along without our help and industries," Stimson calculated, "and we have coming into action a weapon which will be unique."[91] A day later, in his diary, the secretary of war wrote: "Over any such tangled wave [weave] of problems the S-1 secret would be dominant and yet we will not know until after that time probably, until after that meeting whether this is a weapon in our hands or not. We think it will be shortly afterwards, but it seems a terrible thing to gamble with such big stakes in diplomacy without having your *master card* in your hand."[92] This crucial card, for Stimson, was the atomic bomb.

Truman also saw himself as playing atomic poker.[93] He was determined to beat Stalin in the negotiations at Potsdam — "win, lose or draw."[94] Returning on the *Augusta,* Truman received the news of the bombing of Hiroshima. Excitedly, he announced to the officers in the room: "We have just dropped a bomb on Japan which has more power than twenty thousand tons of TNT. It was an overwhelming success. We won the gamble."[95] In a radio broadcast the next day, Truman announced the success of the first atomic bomb: "We have spent two billion dollars on the greatest scientific gamble in history — and won."[96] Later, after the war, a cabinet member told Truman that he still had "an atomic bomb up [his] sleeve" in his negotiations with Russia.[97]

References to knives, guns, cowboys, Indians, and the winning of the West were sprinkled in the conversations and infused into the thinking of the policymakers as they negotiated with Stalin and brandished their new superweapon. The frontier experience, as Frederick Jackson Turner noted, had been a shaping force in American history. However, as it turned out, its legacy was not only democracy but also a propensity for displaying violence.

Truman's favorite saying had frontier origins. On his desk in the White House, Truman had a sign: "The Buck Stops Here." In the old days of the West, poker players often used a knife with a buck-horn handle as a marker to indicate the next dealer. If the player chose not to deal, he would pass the "buck."[98]

The frontier and Indian fighting were part of Truman's family past. His grandfather Solomon Young ran a wagon train from Independence, Missouri, to San Francisco. When the retired president was asked whether his grandfather had had any trouble with the Indians, Truman boasted: "I never heard him say that they bothered him. There were two or three trainmasters that the Indians didn't disturb, and he was one of them.

They were afraid of him. That's why. They knew he had the ammunition and the guns, and he would shoot them if they commenced to bother him."[99] From Grandfather Young, Truman had learned a lesson: Let your enemy know you have the guns.

Similarly, General Leslie Groves proudly viewed the westward movement as a triumph over Indians. He had been instrumental in both the building and dropping of the atomic bomb against Japan. He helped guide the thinking and actions of the Target Committee and the Interim Committee. For Groves, the destruction of Hiroshima ended the war and also served as a warning to the "enemy" — Russia.[100] In his memoir, *Now It Can Be Told: The Story of the Manhattan Project,* he recounted what happened in a staid and controlled way, at times like a military report. But then Groves ended with a personal story: "When I was a boy, I lived with my father at a number of the Army posts that had sprung up during the Indian wars throughout the western United States. There I came to know many of the old soldiers and scouts who had devoted their active lives to the winning of the West. And as I listened to the stories of their deeds, I grew somewhat dismayed, wondering what was left for me to do now that the West was won."[101] Like many American soldiers who saw themselves fighting "Indians" on Pacific islands, Groves found that there was something left for him to do in the winning of the West.

Secretary of State Byrnes also carried a frontier mentality into his power diplomacy with Russia. He saw the war against Japan as a hunt, and he wanted Russia to stay out of it. Press secretary Walter Brown noted that Byrnes was "still hoping for time," believing that the atomic attack would hasten the end of the war and thus Russia would "not get in so much on the kill, thereby being in a position to press for claims against China."[102] Byrnes viewed the atomic bomb as a diplomatic weapon in dealing with Russia. He thought, however, that the bomb should be kept an unstated threat — what he called "the gun behind the door."[103]

Sometimes, however, Byrnes was unable to hide the "ominous bulge in his pocket" and keep the intimidation implicit.[104] At the September 1945 London Conference, Byrnes was provoked by Molotov into an exchange of some humorous remarks suggesting a shootout. The Soviet foreign minister had commented on America's nuclear weapon monopoly and jokingly asked Byrnes if he had an atomic bomb in his side pocket. "You don't know Southerners," Byrnes parried. "We carry our artillery in our hip pocket. If you don't cut out all this stalling and let us get down to work I am going to pull an atomic bomb out of my hip pocket and let you have it." Molotov laughed, nervously.[105]

In a wire to Byrnes, Truman advised him to be tough with the Russians: "Give 'em hell and stand [by] your guns."[106]

On December 21, 1945, the cover of *Time* featured a picture of the president with a mighty fist gripping several lightning bolts superimposed on an exploding mushroom cloud. Harry Truman had been named "Man of the Year."[107]

7

HIROSHIMA: FACES OF WAR AND HUMANITY

> And let me speak to the yet unknowing world
> How these things came about: so shall you hear
> Of carnal, bloody, and unnatural acts,
> Of accidental judgments, casual slaughters,
> Of deaths put on by cunning and forc'd cause,
> And, in this upshot, purposes mistook
> Fall'n on th' inventors' heads: all this can I
> Truly deliver.
>
> Shakespeare, *Hamlet*
>
> (Passage underlined in copy of play in
> Harry S. Truman's private library.)[1]

A Frankenstein

When General George Marshall received the news about Hiroshima from General Leslie Groves, he noted that the bomb had undoubtedly killed a large number of Japanese and cautioned that it would be a mistake to rejoice too much.[2]

Born in 1880 in Uniontown, Pennsylvania, Marshall graduated from the Virginia Military Institute and served in the Philippines, then in Europe during World War I. As army chief of staff under Truman, Marshall had suggested that the first bomb be dropped on a purely military target, like a large naval base. If this action did not force Japan to surrender unconditionally, he argued, then we should warn the Japanese people that several manufacturing areas would be targeted for destruction, but not disclose our choices. "We must offset by such warning methods," Marshall continued, "the opprobrium which might follow from an ill-considered employment of such force."[3]

While Marshall saw that the atomic bomb would help end the war against Japan, he was nervous and uncertain about the decision. Concerned about the postwar security of the nation, he thought that the bomb should not be used. Instead, the United States should keep its existence a secret. "We would be in a stronger position with regard to future military action if we did not show the power we had."[4]

The army chief of staff had tried to bring about a peace with Japan without an atomic attack. He supported the idea of allowing Japan to surrender conditionally, with an explicit U.S. commitment to spare the emperor. From a "purely military point of view," he suggested, we should not demand the removal of the emperor before the termination of hostilities. Marshall thought that the U.S. could use Hirohito to end the fighting by having him order his troops to give up their arms.[5] When he dispatched Truman's order to drop the atomic bomb, Marshall already believed that Japan had lost the war. Shortly before he died, Marshall told an interviewer that the atomic bomb had precipitated the surrender only "by months."[6]

Chairman of the Joint Chiefs of Staff William D. Leahy went even further than General Marshall: the admiral believed that the atomic bomb was not at all necessary. Like Marshall, Leahy had a long career in the military. Born in 1875, he served in the Philippines during the Spanish-American War and then in Europe during World War I. From 1927 to 1931, he was chief of the Navy Bureau of Ordnance. "It is my opinion," he wrote in his memoirs, "that the use of this barbarous weapon at Hiroshima and Nagasaki was of no material assistance in our war against Japan. The Japanese were already defeated and ready to surrender because of the effective sea blockade and the success-ful bombing with conventional weapons." In fact, Leahy had tried to end the war sooner, before Hiroshima. In June, he had urged Truman to accept a Japanese surrender, with provision to allow the emperor to remain, then simply declare an American victory. During the final negotiations on August 10, Leahy suc-cessfully persuaded Truman to accept Japan's surrender offer, with one condition — the retention of the emperor.[7]

Leahy had hoped the United States would not use the atomic bomb in combat. As a soldier, the admiral had definite moral standards on how war should be fought. In July 1944, during a discussion about the use of biological warfare, Leahy "re-coiled" from the idea and told Roosevelt: "Mr. President, this [using germs and poison] would violate every Christian ethic I have ever heard of and all of the known laws of war." Leahy applied this same ethical standard to what was used at Hiro-shima. As a former specialist in gunnery and head of the Bureau of Ordnance, he knew how to judge weapons. " 'Bomb' is the wrong word to use for this new weapon," he wrote. "It is not a bomb. It is not an explosive. It is a poisonous thing that kills people by its deadly radioactive reaction, more than by the ex-plosive force it develops."[8]

The devastation of Hiroshima forced Leahy to realize his own humanity. In his memoirs, he expressed his regret: "My own feeling is that in being the first to use it, we had adopted an ethical standard common to barbarians of the Dark Ages. I was not taught to make war in that fashion, and wars cannot be won by destroying women and children." The atomic bomb, Leahy stated with moral conviction, was a terrible instrument of "uncivilized warfare" — a "modern type of barbarism not worthy of Christian man."[9]

Like Marshall and Leahy, air force commander General Carl Spaatz also had misgivings about Hiroshima. After the war,

Spaatz said that he had been carrying out orders and that the bombings did not bother him. Actually, as the wartime evidence shows, his feelings were complex.[10] When he received the verbal directive to drop the atomic bomb, he insisted that the order must be in writing. This had been his policy for the bombing of any specific town. In his diary, General David M. Schlatter noted that Spaatz was determined that the American air force would not end this war with a "reputation for indiscriminate bombing."[11] When Spaatz received the written order signed by General Marshall and Secretary of War Stimson, he carried it out. But the record would show that he was simply obeying the orders of the men above him.[12]

Furthermore, General Spaatz did not want to bomb Nagasaki. On July 31, he sent a warning to the State Department: "Prisoner-of-war reports, though not verified by photos, give location of Allied prisoner-of-war camp one mile north of center of city of Nagasaki." He then urgently asked: "Does this influence the choice of this target?" The reply came promptly: "Targets previously assigned . . . remain unchanged." As it turned out, the camp housed 1,400 prisoners, most of them Americans.[13] After the bombing of Hiroshima, Spaatz again tried to save Nagasaki. He phoned Washington to suggest that the next atomic weapon be dropped on a less populated area so it "would not be as devastating to the city and the people."[14] Spaatz was instructed to proceed as planned. The bomb fell three miles from the POW camp.

Of the many men around the president who were troubled by the bombing of Hiroshima, probably Secretary of War Henry Stimson experienced the most agonizing introspection. In a sense, he was like Gonzalo, the wise old counselor in Shakespeare's *Tempest*. A graduate of Phillips Andover, Yale College, and Harvard Law School, the seventy-seven-year-old Stimson had served four presidents — as secretary of war under William

Howard Taft, governor of the Philippines under Calvin Coolidge, secretary of state under Herbert Hoover, and secretary of war under Roosevelt. Suddenly finding himself serving a new president, Stimson worried that Truman was not qualified to lead the nation and the world to peace. "I am very sorry for the President," Stimson wrote in his diary on April 23, 1945, "because he is new on his job and he has been brought into a situation which ought not to have been allowed to come in this way." Like Gonzalo, Stimson realized that the atomic bomb had ushered in a "brave new world," filled with "all torment, trouble, wonder, and amazement." Stimson, too, must have hoped that "some heavenly power" would guide humanity out of this "fearful country."[15] As secretary of war and chair of the Interim Committee, Stimson found himself pondering the meaning of what he termed the "colossal reality" of the atomic bomb.[16]

Earlier, Stimson had opposed the expansion of the air war and its indiscriminate mass killings of civilians. He advised Truman that the American air force should confine its bombings to precision targets, partly because he "did not want to have the United States acquire the reputation of outdoing Hitler in atrocities."[17] On February 22, 1945, Stimson stated at a press conference: "Our policy never has been to inflict terror bombing on civilian populations."[18] On May 16, 1945, Stimson informed Truman that he was anxious to hold the air force to "precision bombing" in Japan because "the reputation of the United States for fair play and humanitarianism is the world's biggest asset for peace in the coming decades. . . . The same rule of sparing the civilian population should be applied as far as possible to the use of any new weapon."[19]

During a meeting of the Interim Committee on June 1, 1945, according to J. Robert Oppenheimer, Stimson seemed melancholy. The secretary of war expressed dismay at the "appalling" lack of conscience and compassion ushered in by the war, reported Oppenheimer. Stimson stated that he found disturbing the "complacency, the indifference, and the silence with which we greeted the mass bombings in Europe and, above all, Japan." He said that he could not feel "exultant" about the bombings of Hamburg, Dresden, and Tokyo. "As far as degradation went," Stimson declared, "we had had it; that it would take a new life and a new breath to heal the harm."[20]

Stimson had been brooding over "S-1" — the code term for the atomic bomb. For the June 1 meeting, Stimson had prepared handwritten notes, cryptic and fierce reflections, almost like a poem of despair and dread:

S.1

Its *size* and *character*
We don't think it *mere* new *weapon*
Revolutionary Discovery of Relation of man to universe
Great History Landmark like
　　Gravitation
Copernican Theory
But,
Bids fair [to be] *infinitely greater, respect* to its *Effect*
　— on the ordinary affairs of man's life.
May *destroy* or *perfect* International *Civilization*
May [be] *Frankenstein or* means for World Peace[21]

In the end, the Interim Committee recommended to Truman that the atomic bomb be used against Japan as soon as possible and without warning.

A month later, Stimson tried to end the war before this recommendation could be implemented. In a memorandum to Truman dated July 2, he proposed a plan for peace: "I believe Japan *is* susceptible to reason in such a crisis to a much greater extent than is indicated by our current press and other current comment." A cultured man who had visited Japan on many occasions in the 1920s, Stimson expressed his admiration for the Japanese people: "Japan is not a nation composed wholly of mad fanatics of an entirely different mentality from ours." Refusing to demonize and racialize the enemy, he continued: "On the contrary, she has within the past century shown herself to possess extremely intelligent people, capable in an unprecedentedly short time of adopting not only the complicated technique of Occidental civilization but to a substantial extent their culture and their political and social ideas."

Then the secretary of war proposed a strategy: the United States should give "a carefully timed warning to Japan," which included a conditional surrender. "I personally think that if in [giving such a warning] we should add that we do not exclude a constitutional monarchy under her present dynasty, it would substantially add to the chances of acceptance."[22]

Ten days later, at a meeting with Secretary of the Navy James Forrestal and Undersecretary of State Joseph C. Grew, Stimson said that if American policymakers could accomplish all their strategic objectives without using the phrase "unconditional surrender," they should have "no hesitation" in abandoning the term. Several years after the war, in his memoirs, Stimson admitted that their refusal to modify the unconditional surrender demand might have been a mistake: "History might find that the United States, by its delay in stating its position [on the conditions of surrender], had prolonged the war."[23] Delay had also led to the vaporization of Hiroshima and Nagasaki.

The day after the second atomic blast, Stimson reflected on the tragedy of the avoidable killing of so many people. He was fully aware of Japan's attack on Pearl Harbor, atrocities such as the Bataan Death March, and the bloody battles in the Pacific, but he refused to be driven by a rage for revenge. Stimson did not want to add unnecessarily to the horrors of the war. In his diary, he recalled how at Potsdam he had advocated the "continuance" of the emperorship with certain conditions. "The President and Byrnes struck that out." Then Stimson noted the terrible influence of stereotypes. "There has been a good deal of uninformed agitation against the Emperor in this country mostly by people who know no more about Japan than has been given them by Gilbert and Sullivan's 'Mikado,' and I found today that curiously enough it had gotten deeply embedded in the minds of influential people in the State Department."[24]

At Potsdam, Stimson found himself shut out of the deliberations and negotiations by the State Department, especially by Byrnes. Stimson recognized Byrnes as "very shrewd" and was aware that he was not getting information about the discussions taking place in the "informal conferences." On July 19, Stimson recorded in his diary that Byrnes was "hugging matters in this Conference pretty close to his bosom." Four days later, Stimson noted that Truman and Byrnes were meeting, and complained that he was not included in these discussions. "I am finding myself crippled by not knowing what happens in the meetings in the late afternoon and evening." On July 24, he learned that Byrnes had "preferred not" to include in the Potsdam Declaration Stimson's proposal to offer Japan a conditional surrender. Stimson feared this decision would "mar" the possibility of a Japanese acceptance of surrender.[25]

For Stimson, the atomic bomb was connected to two goals — the need to end the war with Japan and the need to avoid a war with the Soviet Union. The prospect of a nuclear arms race between Russia and the United States had been a nightmare for him. In his diary on December 31, 1944, Stimson recorded his discussion with Roosevelt on this disturbing problem. The "question of troubles with Russia" required American policy-makers to think about "the future of S-1." Stimson had said he was "troubled" about the possible effect of keeping atomic research from the Russians. Yet he had advised continued secrecy, in order to extract concessions from them: "I believed that it was essential not to take them into our confidence until we were sure to get a real *quid pro quo* from our frankness. I said I had no illusions as to the possibility of keeping permanently such a secret but that I did not think it was yet time to share it with Russia." Four months later, in a report dated April 25, Stimson warned that the U.S. would not be able to keep its atomic monopoly. In fact, he argued, it was "practically certain that we could not remain in this position indefinitely." Then he apprehensively predicted: "Probably the only nation that could enter into production within the next few years is Russia."[26]

The blasts at Hiroshima and Nagasaki shook Stimson and forced him to re-evaluate his entire Russian strategy of a quid pro quo, with the U.S. holding the "master card." Now he felt that this approach was "wrong," and that the U.S. should do everything it could to prevent an atomic arms race. Stimson was convinced the U.S. should share nuclear technology with the Soviet Union.[27]

One month after Hiroshima, Stimson advised Truman: "The only way you can make a man trustworthy is to trust him; and the surest way to make him untrustworthy is to distrust him and show your distrust." Stimson explained the reversal of his thinking. He still wanted to help Russian society understand the value of "individual liberty," but he had come to the conclusion that the atomic bomb could not be used to bring about such political and cultural reform. "I have become convinced," the elder diplomat told Truman, "that any demand by us for an internal change in Russia as a condition of sharing in the atomic weapon would be so resented that it would make the objective we have in view less probable." American policymakers should no longer, Stimson urged, confront the Russians with the atomic bomb "ostentatiously on [their] hip." The transformation of Russian society would come slowly, and the U.S. government should not delay pursuing a cooperative approach. "I believe that this long process of change in Russia is more likely to be expedited by the closer relationship in the matter of the atomic bomb. . . ."[28]

Shortly after this meeting with Truman, Stimson resigned as secretary of war and retreated to his home at Highhold, one of the locations mentioned in the top secret message carrying the news about Alamogordo. A year and a half later, he wrote an essay published in *Harper's Magazine* to explain why America had used the atomic bomb against Japan. As it turned out, his account was confusing and sometimes even self-contradictory. While describing the events leading up to the bombing of Hiroshima, Stimson frequently interrupted his narrative with references to the "omnious threat" of Russia, the "two schools of thought" regarding the control of the new weapon in the postwar world, and the danger of destroying modern civilization. In effect, Stimson was acknowledging that the reason for dropping the bomb had not been simply to end the war without an invasion and thereby save American lives.[29]

Perhaps the twists and turns in the essay were inadvertent, unconscious, betraying a hidden ambivalence. A brilliant individual, trained as lawyer, Stimson did not allow his conflicted thoughts and emotions to pass unnoticed, at least not by himself. He concluded his essay with some puzzling and painful reflections:

"As I read over what I have written, I am aware that much of it, in this year of peace, may have a harsh and unfeeling sound. It would perhaps be possible to say the same things and say them more gently. But I do not think it would be wise. As I look back over the five years of my service as Secretary of War, I see too many stern and heart-rending decisions to be willing to pretend that war is anything else than what it is. The face of war is the face of death; death is an inevitable part of every order that a wartime leader gives. . . . In this last great action of the Second World War we were given final proof that war is death. War in the twentieth century has grown steadily more barbarous, more destructive, more debased in all its aspects."[30]

A Matter of Moral Importance

Many of the atomic scientists had begun thinking about the implications of their creation long before the explosion at Alamogordo. On November 18, 1944, a group of them, led by Enrico Fermi and James Franck, offered ominious scenarios of an atomic future. They pointed out that the British, Germans, and Russians were also actively engaged in nuclear-weapons research. In the postwar era, they said, the U.S. should try to maintain its lead in this field. But they doubted that this policy would ensure lasting security against a global castastrophe. Unless a central international authority were established to control nuclear power, they warned, nations armed with atomic bombs would unleash them against one another in "senseless mutual destruction."[31]

In a top secret memorandum dated June 26, 1945, George Harrison, of the Interim Committee, informed Stimson that many of the atomic scientists were concerned about the dangers of nuclear power. Doubtful that a safe system of international control could be established, they envisaged an atomic arms race that would threaten civilization. Several scientists at the Chicago Metallurgical Laboratory, Harrison reported, opposed the use of the bomb against Japan. They felt that if the U.S. deployed the new weapon it would sacrifice the country's "whole moral position." Without ethical credibility, it would be difficult for the United States to propose or enforce any system of international control designed to make this tremendous force an influence toward "world peace rather than an uncontrollable weapon of war."[32] In short, an atomic attack on Japan could open a Pandora's box leading to the obliteration of the world.

About two weeks later, on July 11, 1945, Franck and Leo Szilard formally presented a report on the issue. They argued that the decision on the use of the bomb should not be left in the hands of the military. The "highest political leadership" should also weigh the issue very carefully. "If we consider international agreement on total prevention of nuclear warfare as the paramount objective, and believe that it can be achieved, this kind of introduction of atomic weapons to the world may easily destroy all our chances of success."[33]

They suggested a display of the bomb's might rather than an actual combat use. A "demonstration" of the bomb "before the eyes of representatives of all the United Nations, on the desert or a barren island," Franck and Szilard argued, would give the government the opportunity to find out what American "public opinion" might be on the question of whether the weapon should be deployed against Japan. They noted that it was "not at all certain that American public opinion, if it could be enlightened as to the effect of atomic explosives, would approve of our own country being the first to introduce such an indiscriminate method of wholesale destruction of civilian life."[34]

Looking ahead at the probability of the bomb's deployment, Franck and Szilard predicted that a nuclear arms race would begin immediately after an atomic attack on Japan: "If no efficient international agreement is achieved, the race for nuclear armaments will be on in earnest not later than the morning after our first demonstration of the existence of nuclear weapons."[35]

Szilard was the leader of the scientists' efforts to try to stop the train of events pushing the world toward Hiroshima. An atomic attack might hasten the end of the war, Szilard argued, but it would also lead directly to an extremely volatile confrontation with the Soviet Union. "Perhaps the greatest immediate danger which faces us is the probability that our 'demonstration' of atomic bombs will precipitate a race in the production of these devices between the United States and Russia."[36]

This danger had alarmed Szilard even before the explosion at Alamogordo. In a March 12, 1945, memo on "Atomic Bombs and the Postwar Position of the United States," Szilard advised President Roosevelt that the country had a choice: enter into an atomic arms agreement with Russia or be forced to compete in an atomic arms race. Szilard predicted that the Soviets would be able to make atomic bombs within six years. "After this war," he warned, "it is conceivable that it will become possible to drop atomic bombs on cities in the United States from very great distances by means of rockets." Exhibiting singular foresight, the scientist offered a horrifying scenario. The "greatest danger" would be the possibility of the outbreak of "a *preventive war*." Such a war might be the outcome of the fear that the other country might strike first.[37] Thus, bristling with nuclear weapons pointed at one another, either the U.S. or the Soviet Union might initiate a surprise atomic attack in order to protect itself from nuclear annihilation.

Szilard wanted to give his memo directly to Roosevelt, but he felt he needed an endorsement from Albert Einstein. "Since I didn't suppose that he would know who I was, I needed a letter of introduction."[38] However, Szilard was never able to get his message to Roosevelt. The scientist then tried to see Truman, the new president, who told him to discuss his concerns with James Byrnes, a member of the Interim Committee. His May 28 meeting went badly. Byrnes wanted the U.S. to keep its atomic monopoly in order to intimidate Soviet leaders and make the Soviet Union more manageable. Szilard left the meeting feeling depressed. On July 3, he learned that Byrnes had become the new secretary of state.

Certain the military would use the atomic bomb against Japan, Szilard decided that he and his fellow atomic scientists should forthrightly declare their moral opposition to such action. Szilard drafted a petition to Truman. "However small the chance might be that our petition may influence the course of events," he wrote to a colleague on July 4, "I personally feel that it would be a *matter of importance* if a large number of scientists who have worked in this field went clearly and unmistakably on record as to their opposition on moral grounds to the use of these bombs in the present phase of the war" (italics added).[39] Szilard admitted to his fellow scientists that the petition would be futile. But, he argued in letters to several scientists, "from a point of view of the standing of the scientists in the eyes of the general public one or two years from now it is a good thing that a minority of scientists should have gone on record in favor of giving greater weight to moral arguments and should have exercised their right given to them by the Constitution to petition the President. . . ."[40]

Szilard's petition prompted the Manhattan Project directors to take a poll of the atomic scientists. In July, 150 scientists were asked whether and how the weapon should be used against Japan. The options were:

1. Use the weapons in the manner that is from the military point of view most effective in bringing about prompt Japanese surrender at minimum cost to our armed forces.
2. Give a military demonstration in Japan, to be followed by a renewed opportunity for surrender before full use of the weapon is employed.
3. Give an experimental demonstration in this country, with

representatives of Japan present; followed by a new opportunity for surrender before full use of the weapons is employed.

4. Withhold military use of the weapons, but make public experimental demonstration of their effectiveness.
5. Maintain as secret as possible all development of our new weapons, and refrain from using them in this war.

Only fifteen percent voted for number 1. Forty-six percent voted for number 2, twenty-six percent for number 3, eleven percent for number 4, and two percent for number 5. Thus, eighty-five percent of the scientists had voted against the way the bomb would actually be used at Hiroshima and Nagasaki — the surprise "full use" of the bomb.[41]

On July 13, 1945, the poll's results were transmitted to Arthur Compton, project leader of the Chicago laboratory. Three days later, the first atomic bomb was exploded at Alamogordo. On July 24, in a memo to Colonel K. D. Nichols, who worked under General Groves, Compton forwarded Szilard's "A Petition Addressed to the President of the United States," dated July 17. Sixty-seven scientists signed the petition and went on record. They declared

Discoveries of which the people of the United States are not aware may affect the welfare of this nation in the near future. The liberation of atomic power which has been achieved places atomic bombs in the hands of the Army. It places in your hands, as Commander-in-Chief, the fateful decision whether or not to sanction the use of such bombs in the present phase of the war against Japan. . . .

The war has to be brought speedily to a successful conclusion and attacks by atomic bombs may very well be an effective method of warfare. We feel, however, that such attacks on Japan could not be justified, at least not unless the terms which will be imposed after the war on Japan were made public in detail and Japan were given an opportunity to surrender. . . .

The development of atomic power will provide the nations with new means of destruction. The atomic bombs at our disposal represent only the first step in this direction, and there is almost no limit to the destructive power which will become available in the course of future development. Thus a nation which sets the precedent of using these newly liberated forces of nature for purposes of destruction may have to bear the responsibility of opening the door to an era of devastation on an unimaginable scale. . . .

In view of the foregoing, we, the undersigned, respectfully petition: first, that you exercise your power as Commander-in-Chief, to rule that the United States shall not resort to the use of atomic bombs in this war unless the terms which will be imposed upon Japan have been made public in detail and Japan knowing these terms has refused to surrender; second, that in such an event the question whether or not to use atomic bombs be decided by you in the light of the considerations presented in this petition as well as all the other moral responsibilities which are involved.[42]

General Groves received the petition on July 25 but held onto it until August 1, when he finally forwarded it to Stimson. The secretary of war was still at Potsdam and did not see the petition until after he had returned to the United States in August.

By then, it was too late. Hiroshima had happened. On August 6, Szilard wrote to his close friend and future wife, Trude Weiss: "I suppose you have seen to-day's newspapers. Using atomic bombs against Japan is one of the greatest blunders of history. Both from a practical point of view on a ten-years scale and from the point of view of our moral position. — I went out of my way (and very much so) in order to prevent it but, as today's papers show, without success. It is very difficult to see what wise course of action is possible from here on."[43]

Szilard had first warned Roosevelt about Nazi atomic research in 1939, and he later tried to stop the American atomic project. He believed that Byrnes was taking the United States and the world down a dangerous path. "I thought to myself," Szilard remarked after Hiroshima, "how much better off the world might be had I been born in America and become influential in American politics, and had Byrnes been born in Hungary and studied physics. In all probability there would then have been no atomic bomb and no danger of an arms race between America and Russia."[44]

Remembering how he had been persuaded by Szilard to warn Roosevelt about the potential Nazi nuclear threat and advise the president that the U.S. should initiate atomic research, Albert Einstein wrote to Linus Pauling after Hiroshima: "I made one great mistake in my life, when I signed the letter to President Roosevelt recommending that atom bombs be made. . . ."[45]

The attack on Hiroshima stirred waves of remorse among many Manhattan Project scientists. When the *Enola Gay* left on its mission, Philip Morrison was at Tinian, preparing the bomb that would be dropped on Nagasaki. "We heard the news of Hiroshima from the airplane itself, a coded message," he recalled. "When they returned, we didn't see them [the crew]. The generals had them. But then the people came back with photographs. I remember looking at them with awe and terror. We knew something terrible had been unleashed. The men had a great party that night to celebrate, but we didn't go. Almost no physicists went to it. We obviously killed a hundred thousand people and that was nothing to party about."[46]

When he heard the news about Hiroshima, atomic scientist John Grove exclaimed: "Thank God we really were successful. That proves that all the money that was spent on the project was worthwhile." But then the impact of the event hit him. "About two seconds later it struck home. 'Oh my God, Hiroshima. They dropped the atomic bomb on a city.'" Grove became angry: "Why a city? Why didn't they drop it on the great naval base at Truk, or some other military installation? God knows how many people they've killed. Maybe a hundred thousand, maybe five hundred thousand."[47]

More than anyone else, J. Robert Oppenheimer had helped perfect the bomb. In 1945, Oppenheimer was still a young man, only forty-one years old. The son of immigrants from Germany, he was born in New York City and received his A.B. from Harvard and his Ph.D. from the University of Göttingen. Philosophically inclined, he was also perspicacious. Years earlier, on August 10, 1931, he had written to his brother, Frank: "I think that the world in which we shall live in these next thirty years will be a pretty restless and tormented place; I do not think that there will be much of a compromise possible between being of it, and being not of it."[48]

Oppenheimer had been drawn away from a physics professorship at the University of California, Berkeley, to become director of the Los Alamos weapons laboratory. In the vastness of the New Mexican desert, he had orchestrated an amazing and brilliant feat. He had directed an army of scientists and technicians in a superhuman effort to assemble and test the first atomic bomb. Oppenheimer inspired them with a sense of purpose, and, as they built the bomb, they created a feeling of community. After work, they relaxed together and shared stories. During one of these times, Edward U. Condon read aloud passages from *The Tempest*, a seemingly fitting text. Like Prospero, they were exiled, this time in a desert; they, too, had a mission in a brave new world. They would command Ariel, atomic technology, to move the heavens and the earth.[49]

Oppenheimer did more than lead the effort to build the bomb: he also helped decide how it would be used. As a member of Groves's Target Committee and an adviser to the Interim

Committee, Oppenheimer had supported the recommendation to deploy the bomb in combat against Japan.[50]

But Oppenheimer felt a vexing uncertainty about unleashing this "shatterer of worlds." On August 6, 1945, he received a phone call from General Groves. The Manhattan Project director said that the bomb had gone off with a "tremendous bang," and that he was glad he had selected Oppenheimer as the Los Alamos director. His choice had been "one of the wisest things" he had ever done, Groves remarked. "Well," Oppenheimer replied, "I have my doubts, General Groves."[51]

After the bomb was dropped on Hiroshima, Oppenheimer felt moral revulsion. He reported having "terrible moral scruples" about the killing of 70,000 people at Hiroshima.[52] Oppenheimer was facing the question raised by people like the German Jesuit priest Father Siemes, who was in Japan during Hiroshima: "The crux of the matter is whether total war in its present form is justifiable, even when it serves a just purpose."[53]

On October 16, Oppenheimer stepped down as director of Los Alamos. The entire weapons-laboratory community gathered to honor him at a ceremony; General Groves presented the Secretary of War's Certificate of Appreciation to the leader of the bomb project. During the celebration, dime-sized sterling silver pins were distributed: each one was stamped with a large "A" and a small "BOMB." University of California president Robert G. Sproul was present to accept recognition for his institution's contribution. At the conclusion of the ceremony, the Army chaplain offered a prayer and declared: "Oh God, bless all schools and colleges, and especially the University of California."[54]

Oppenheimer himself did not share the euphoria of the moment. In fact, he lent a somberness to the event. In the middle of the ceremony, he gave a short speech. Under the New Mexico sky, which had earlier witnessed a sudden burst of "several suns in midday,"[55] he wondered how the achievement of Los Alamos would be remembered by future generations: "If atomic bombs are to be added as new weapons to the arsenals of a warring world, or to the arsenals of nations preparing for war, then the time will come when mankind will curse the names of Los Alamos and Hiroshima."[56]

A month later, Oppenheimer spoke to the Association of Los Alamos Scientists. He reminded them about their responsibility to mankind. "I think there are issues which are quite simple and quite deep, and which involve us as a group of scientists — involve us more, perhaps, than any other group in the world." Oppenheimer reflected on the meaning of total war. He rejected the arguments that war was terrible and that the atomic bomb was "just another weapon." He urged his fellow scientists to recognize that this explosive invention constituted not "just a slight modification" to warfare, but a fundamental change. International control of this new and dangerous force was urgently needed. "The only unique end can be a world that is united," Oppenheimer declared, "and a world in which war will not occur." To do this, he cautioned, Americans would have to embrace their humanity — their "common bond with other men everywhere."[57]

A Laguna Pueblo Indian would later write about the atomic blast at Alamogordo, only a few hundred miles from her reservation. In her novel *Ceremony*, Leslie Marmon Silko looked at a ceremonial sand painting and saw the tragedy of the event. "From that time on, human beings were one clan again, united by the fate the destroyers had planned for them, for all living things; united by a circle of death that devoured people in cities twelve thousand miles away. . . ."[58]

But for many people, that very circle also created a sense of connectedness to one another as human beings.

The Holocaust and Hiroshima

The day after the bombing of Hiroshima, Hanson W. Baldwin of the *New York Times* described the shock he felt: "Yesterday man unleashed the atom to destroy man, and another chapter in human history opened, a chapter in which the weird, the strange, the horrible becomes the trite and the obvious. Yesterday we clinched victory in the Pacific, but we sowed the whirlwind." Baldwin pointed out that the atomic attack was a logical culmination of the escalating air war. "Much of our bombing throughout this war — like the enemy's — has been directed against cities and hence against civilians. Because our bombing has been more effective and hence more devastating, Americans have become a synomyn for destruction." Baldwin then warned: "We have been the first to introduce a new weapon of unknowable effects which may bring us victory quickly but which will sow the seeds of hate more widely than ever. We may yet reap the whirlwind."[59]

Two weeks later, in a sober essay in *Life* entitled "The Atomic Bomb and Future War," Baldwin spelled out how that whirlwind had altered our humanity: "In a fraction of a second on Aug. 5, 1945, American scientists not only destroyed Hiroshima, Japan, but with it many human concepts — chief among them our ideas of how to wage war." While the United States now had to prepare for atomic warfare, Baldwin concluded, it also needed to search for alternatives to war itself. We had to realize that this was "One World" and that we must establish "a common brotherhood or die in droves beneath the atomic bombs."[60] Baldwin's message was clear. The new weapon had offered us a choice: either unity or annihilation.

Shortly after Hiroshima, *Time* also wondered what we had won. The victory was one of "sorrow and doubt as with joy and gratitude," the editors wrote. "In what they said and did, men are still, as the aftershock of a great wound, bemused and only semi-articulate, whether they were soldiers or scientists, or great statesmen, or the simplest of men. But in the dark depths of their minds and hearts, huge forms moved and silently arrayed themselves: Titans, arranging out of the chaos an age in which victory was already only the shout of a child in the street." The editors welcomed the end of the war. "But the demonstration of power against living creatures instead of dead matter," they declared with regret, "created a bottomless wound in the living conscience of the race." The war's outcome seemed the "most grimly Pyrrhic of victories."[61]

Similarly, on August 20, *Life* expressed deep disquietude. "The Second World War, which had been tapering off to a whimper," the editors observed, "is ending instead with a bang." They harshly criticized the sharp rise in the destructiveness of the air war since the late 1930s. "From the very concept of strategic bombing, all the developments — night, pattern, saturation, area, indiscriminate — have led straight to Hiroshima, and Hiroshima was, and was intended to be, almost pure *Schrecklichkeit* [terror bombing]." What we needed to fear the most today, the editors warned, was not the atom but the nature of man. "No limits are set to our Promethean ingenuity, provided we remember we are not Jove. We are not ants either; we can abolish warfare, and mitigate man's inhumanity to man. But all this will take some doing. And we are in a strange new land."[62]

Americans had no knowledge of the atomic bomb before it was dropped on Hiroshima, and many of them were appalled. A citizen from St. Paul asked: "Why . . . did we choose to drop our first bomb on a crowded city, where 90% of the casualties would *inevitably be civilian?*"[63] On September 27, 1945, former president Herbert Hoover told a conference of newspaper editors: "Despite any sophistries its major use is not to kill fighting men, but to kill women, children, and civilian men of whole cities as a pressure on governments. If it comes into general use, we may see all civilization destroyed."[64]

We had, many Americans thought, deployed a weapon without mercy on innocent civilians. "The bomb dropped on Hiroshima was a big terrible thing," a woman from Kentucky recalled later, "but I didn't know it was the horror it was. It was on working people. It wasn't anywhere near the big shots of Japan who started the war in the first place. We didn't drop it on them. Hirohito and his white horse, it never touched him. It was dropped on women and children who had nothing to say about whether their country went to war or not."[65]

In a personal letter to her president on August 9, 1945, Anne Ford protested against the use of the bomb: "I think it is a disgrace that America should be involved in such a diabolical thing. America that was to give example to the rest of the world. . . . I had hoped and prayed that America under your leadership would be a good example to the rest of the world. I don't know what to think now."[66] In letters to the *New York Times,* readers wrote that the atomic attack was "a stain upon our national life" and "simply mass murder, sheer terrorism."[67] Similarly, a woman from New York wrote to Truman: "I am impelled to write to you now and tell you how stunned and sick at heart I am over what our country has just done to Japan and her people — thousands of them innocent."[68]

Others likened the atomic horror to the Nazi holocaust. In a letter to the editor of *Time,* Walter G. Taylor of New York City wrote: "The United States of America has this day become the new master of brutality, infamy, atrocity. Bataan, Buchenwald, Dachau, Coventry, Lidice were tea parties compared with the horror which we, the people of the United States of America, have dumped on the world in the form of atomic energy bombs. No peacetime applications of this Frankenstein monster can ever erase the crime we have committed. . . . It is no democracy where such an outrage can be committed without our consent!"[69]

Fighting for democracy had particular meaning for African Americans: many blacks viewed World War II as a struggle for "Double Victory" — over fascism abroad and racism at home. W. E. B. DuBois defined the defense of America as a "War for Racial Equality" and a struggle for "democracy not only for white folks but for yellow, brown, and black."[70] In the *Chicago Defender,* a national black newspaper, DuBois condemned the racist way the U.S. had fought the war against the "colored nation" of Japan: "No matter how we explain and assess the damage, the result of thinking along the lines of race and color will affect human relations for many years and will excuse contempt and injustice toward colored skins." DuBois then criticized the atomic attack on Hiroshima: "We have seen in this war, to our amazement and distress, a marriage between science and destruction; a marriage such as we had never dreamed before. We have always thought of science as the emancipator. We see it now as the enslaver of mankind."[71] More blunt than DuBois in her language, black novelist Zora Neale Hurston castigated Truman as a "monster": "I can think of him as nothing else but the Butcher of Asia."[72]

Of Termites and Machines

After the war, Truman repeatedly denied feeling sorry about his decision to drop the atomic bombs on Japanese cities. When asked in an interview whether the decision was a morally difficult one to make, Truman shot back: "Hell no, I made it like that," as he snapped his fingers.[73] Regret appeared to be something Truman refused to allow himself. "Never, never waste a minute on regret," he adamantly declared. "It is a waste of time."[74] Truman insisted that he made decisions with "no regrets, no looking back, no wondering if-I-had-to-do-it-all-over-again would I have?" Dean Acheson wrote that Harry Truman was totally without what he called "that most enfeebling of emotions, regret." An old friend, Ethel Noland, recalled: "The Trumans have never been a lamenting people." Truman believed that a man should just try to do his best. "That's right," he said. "That's the main thing. A man can't do anything more than that. You can't think about how it would be . . . . if you had done another thing. You have to decide." As a retired president, Truman was asked whether he had ever looked back and wished he had done something different when he was in office. "No. Never," Truman replied sharply. "Not one time that I can recall. What would be the use of it?"[75]

Truman especially refused to review what had happened at Potsdam. At this conference, when he learned about the successful Alamogordo explosion, the president decided to use the atomic bomb against Japan. In a sense, the decision had already been made, even before his meeting with Stalin. The fear of a Soviet military threat in the postwar world and the anticipated possession of the powerful new weapon drove Truman toward Byrnes's "monopoly strategy." The demand for "unconditional surrender," which was an inflexible obstacle to ending the war, had become inextricably fastened to the racialized war in the Pacific. This requirement destroyed the possibility of a negotiated peace. New air technologies had created capabilities for massive destruction of cities and raised the levels of so-called permissible violence. Meanwhile, the Manhattan Project had developed a momentum of its own, with its cosmos of laboratories and weapons facilities located across the country, its bureaucracy, its top secret Interim Committee, and its director who saw Russia as the "enemy."[76] This complex and dynamic crisscrossing of circumstances and forces was propelling the country toward what Groves called a "battle test" against Japan.[77]

As it turned out, Truman did not have what Groves called sufficient "nerve" to resist this momentum.[78] Though he alone possessed the authority to make the decision, Truman lacked the enormous strength and self-confidence needed to resist the pressures of men like Groves and Byrnes. Inexperienced and insecure in his role as president, he found himself unable to say "no" to the tough-minded general and the "assistant President."[79] It would have been particularly difficult for Truman to have stood up to the secretary of state. Truman and Byrnes were friends, getting together socially and joking about dressing up like "nigga preachers."[80] Truman also viewed the "conniving" Byrnes as a competitor: he had "accidentally" taken away the vice-presidential nomination from the South Carolina politician.[81] Determined to show the men around him and the world that he was not a "sissy," Truman practiced masculine diplomacy, driven by a culture formed on the frontier.

Reinforcing all these circumstances and influences was race. Like most Americans, Truman had grown up and lived in a society where racial stereotypes were ubiquitous. He had had little opportunity in school or in his community to acquire an accurate understanding of peoples of different races and cultures. Consequently, Truman succumbed to the raging hate rooted in a long history of animosity against the Japanese, as well as the fierce memory of Pearl Harbor.

While he had prejudices, Truman was aware of the fact that America, despite its history of racism, stood for certain great principles that had been forged in the American Revolution and the crucible of the Civil War. Truman understood, as had President Lincoln, that this nation had been "conceived in liberty and dedicated to the proposition that all men are created equal." Like Lincoln, he saw that the struggle to realize this proposition was still "unfinished work."[82] World War II was forcing Americans to reconnect themselves to their country's democratic identity: Nazism, with its ideology of Aryan racial supremacy, was compelling Americans to rededicate themselves to their nation's highest principles.[83]

President Roosevelt understood this imperative when he framed the country's war purpose: the United States was the "arsenal of democracy." America stood for the "four freedoms" — freedom of speech, freedom of worship, freedom from want, and freedom from fear. Our commitment to these freedoms, Roosevelt explained, buttressed America's condemnation of racism. "The principle on which this country was founded and by which it has always been governed is that Americanism is a matter of mind and heart. Americanism is not, and never was, a matter of race or ancestry." Truman, too, reaffirmed these American ideals. When President Truman welcomed home the Japanese-American soldiers of the 442nd Regimental Combat Team, he told them: "You fought for the free nations of the world . . . you fought not only the enemy, you fought prejudice — and you won."[84]

As a boy, Truman had been taught these American ideals of democracy and equality, as well as the importance of personal integrity. Commenting on his mother, he said: "She was always a woman who did the right thing, and she taught us, my brother and sister and I, that, too." A plain farmer from Missouri, Truman saw himself as a decent and honest man. Referring to his early life in Independence, the retired president recalled: "In those days, in the time I was growing up and when I was a young man, people thought more of an honest man than any one thing. . . ." Judge Albert A. Ridge confirmed Truman's memory about the value of honesty in small-town Missouri. "Harry Truman grew up in a society in which a man's word was his bond. If a man's word could be trusted there was no place he couldn't go. Nobody around here ever doubted Harry Truman's word." This trust also had to be with oneself. Truman remembered advice from "Old Tom Jefferson": "Whenever you do a thing, though it can never be known but to yourself, ask yourself how you would act were all the world watching you, and act accordingly."[85]

After the destruction of Hiroshima and Nagasaki, Truman showed a seemingly inordinate need to justify his decision, again and again, suggesting that it had become a nagging reference point of his life. Truman's insecurity had made him anxious about making mistakes as president. On May 8, 1945, he wrote to his mother and sister from his new home in the White House: "Things have moved at a terrific rate here since April 12. Never a day has gone by that some momentous decision didn't have to be made. So far luck has been with me. I hope it keeps up. It can't stay with me forever however and I hope when the mistake comes it won't be too great to remedy."[86]

Years later, interviewer Merle Miller asked Truman directly: "What do you consider the biggest mistake you made as President?" Truman answered that it was the nomination of Thomas C. Clark to the Supreme Court. Miller was disappointed. "I had hoped that when Mr. Truman began considering the biggest mistake he had made as President he might have something new to say about dropping the Bomb. . . ." Miller then commented: "If there was one subject on which Mr. Truman was not going to have any second thoughts, it was the Bomb. If he'd said it once, he said it a hundred times, almost always the same words. The Bomb ended the war. If we had to invade Japan, half a million soldiers on both sides would have been killed. . . . It was as simple as that. That was all there was to it, and Mr. Truman had never lost any sleep over *that* decision."[87]

Truman's defensiveness about his decision surfaced on another occasion. In 1961–2, Miller was doing a documentary program on Truman and was planning to ask him to do an on-camera interview in Hiroshima. Truman and Miller were in conversation when one of the producers said: "Tell the President your idea for the atom-bomb film [the segment of the documentary program]." Truman looked at Miller with "quick suspicion." Awkwardly, Miller explained his desire to film the basic framework for the program's segment on the bomb in Hiroshima. "It was the first time I ever saw him blink," Miller reported. "He was silent for a moment . . . and then he said something surprising to me. . . ." "I'll go to Japan if that's what you want. But I won't kiss their ass."[88]

Truman felt the same way about his American critics, especially Oppenheimer. Several months after the atomic bombings, Truman had a private conversation with the former Los Alamos director, who expressed his deep remorse over Hiroshima. He told Truman that his work at the weapons laboratory meant he had blood on his hands. Truman offered his handkerchief and sneered: "Well, here, would you like to wipe off your hands."[89] Then Truman snapped: "The blood is on my hands. Let me worry about that."[90] After Oppenheimer left the Oval Office, Truman told Dean Acheson: "I don't want to see that son of a bitch in this office ever again."[91] On May 3, 1946, he complained again to Acheson about Oppenheimer: "He came to my office five or six months ago, and spent most of his time wringing his hands and telling me they had blood on them because of the discovery of atomic energy." To Truman, the scientist was a "cry baby."[92] But his reaction to Oppenheimer seemed defensive and shrill.

On August 9, after he had been urged to destroy Japan completely, Truman responded soberly in a private letter: "I know that Japan is a terribly cruel and uncivilized nation in warfare but I can't bring myself to believe that, because they are beasts, we should ourselves act in that same manner. For myself I certainly regret the necessity of wiping out whole populations because of the 'pigheadedness' of leaders of a nation, and, for your information, I am not going to do it unless it is absolutely necessary. My object is to save as many American lives as possible but I also have a humane feeling for the women and children in Japan."[93]

That very day, however, an atomic bomb destroyed Nagasaki. At Potsdam, Truman had told Stimson he hoped only one bomb would be dropped.[94] He had not expected a second bomb to be dropped so soon after the attack on Hiroshima, and immediately ordered the military not to drop a third bomb. He told Henry Wallace that "the thought of wiping out another 100,000 people was too horrible." He did not like the idea of killing "all those kids."[95] For days afterward, Truman complained of terrible headaches. Wallace asked: "Physical or figurative?" Truman replied: "Both."[96]

Truman's anguish was understandable. A thoughtful and sensitive man, he had seen that the world was hurtling toward an uncertain and fearful future. On July 16, while waiting for word from Alamogordo, Truman described in his diary the "absolute ruin" he had witnessed in Berlin on his way to Potsdam and the terrible scenes of war refugees — old men, old women, children, carrying their belongings to nowhere in particular.[97] Philosophically, Truman then recorded his anguished reflections on the world's long, grim history of warfare: "I thought of Carthage, Baalbek, Jerusalem, Rome, Atlantis, Peking, Babylon, Nineveh; Scipio, Rameses II, Titus, Herman, Sherman, Jenghis [sic] Khan, Alexander, Darius the Great. But Hitler only destroyed Stalingrad — and Berlin." Then Truman turned to the war that still had to be ended — and also, perhaps, to the escalating tensions with Stalin and the Soviet Union. "I hope for some sort of peace — but I fear that machines are ahead of morals by some centuries and when morals catch up perhaps there'll be no reason for any of it. I hope not. But we are only termites on a planet and maybe when we bore too deeply into the planet there'll [be] a reckoning — who knows?"[98]

At that very moment at a forlorn and fateful New Mexican desert test site called Trinity, a machine was racing ahead, and men were boring deeply into the planet. Two days later, Truman returned to his diary: "Discussed Manhattan (it is a success)."[99]

NOTES

CHAPTER I. "A PAST THAT IS NOT EVEN PAST"

1. "Rack" means a "wisp of cloud." *The New York Times*, in an editorial, "One Victory Not Yet Won," August 12, 1945, p. 8, found Prospero's statement relevant to describe Hiroshima. Noted in Paul Boyer, *By the Bomb's Early Light: American Thought and Culture at the Dawn of the Atomic Age* (Chapel Hill, 1994), p. 248.

2. Lieutenant General Leslie R. Groves, interview transcript, October 20, 1969, p. 6, MacArthur Memorial Archive, Norfolk, Virginia.

3. Brigadier General LeGrande Diller, interview transcript, "American Caesar," *Cineworld*, 9/26/82, p. 17, MacArthur Memorial Archive; D. Clayton James, *Years of MacArthur: Volume II, 1941–1945* (Boston, 1975), p. 775. James interviewed MacArthur after the war. "Actually, the general felt that the use of atomic bombs at that stage 'was completely unnecessary from a military point of view' to compel Japan's capitulation and said so on several occasions in later years." The thesis that the bombing of Hiroshima and Nagasaki was "unnecessary" is "invincibly correct," wrote Douglas MacArthur to Herbert Hoover. "The Japanese were beaten and seeking peace long before the bombs were dropped." October 8, 1959, MacArthur Memorial Archive.

4. Horace A. Thompson, Jr., letter to Mrs. Douglas MacArthur, August 9, 1994; Thompson, "The Final Days of the War," New Orleans *Times-Picayune,* August 6, 1994, both in MacArthur Memorial Archive.

5. W. E. Rhoades, interview transcript, sound roll 3, camera roll 5, pp. 5–6, MacArthur Memorial Archive.

6. Lance Morrow, "Hiroshima and the Time Machine," *Time,* September 19, 1994, p. 94.

7. Robert H. Ferrell (ed.), *Off the Record: The Private Papers of Harry S. Truman* (New York, 1980). "The President's diary entries for the

Potsdam Conference itself — his experiences in the former German capital — were not discovered until 1979." p. 50.

8. Henry L. Stimson, "The Decision to Use the Atomic Bomb," *Harper's Magazine,* vol. 194, no. 1161, February 1947, pp. 97–107; Harry Truman, *Memoirs of Harry S. Truman: Year of Decisions* (New York: 1986, originally published in 1955–56); James F. Byrnes, *Speaking Frankly* (New York, 1947); Leslie R. Groves, *Now It Can Be Told: The Story of the Manhattan Project* (New York, 1962). Stimson wrote in his introduction: "In recent months there has been much comment about the decision to use atomic bombs in attacks on the Japanese cities of Hiroshima and Nagasaki. This decision was one of the gravest made by our government in recent years, and it is entirely proper that it should be widely discussed. I have therefore decided to record for all who may be interested my understanding of the events which led up to the attack." p. 97. Truman in his preface wrote: "As for myself, I should like to record, before it is too late, as much of the story of my occupancy of the White House as I am able to tell. The events, as I saw them and as I put them down here, I hope may prove helpful in informing some people and in setting others straight on the facts." p. ix. Byrnes said in his foreword: "I have tried, in short, to give you a seat at the conference table. Some critics may say it is too early for these facts to be made known. My answer is that if it were possible to give the people of this world an actual, rather than a figurative, seat at the conference table, the fears and worries that now grip our hearts would fade away." p. xii. Groves stated in his foreword: "In writing this story, I have tried first of all to fill in as many as possible of the gaps existing in the American public's understanding of the project. Altogether too many of these gaps have given rise to misinformed conjecture, and as a result many Americans tend to feel embarrassed or discomfited by their country's greatest single scientific success." p. x. Clearly, all of them had reasons for telling us their stories of what happened.

9. William D. Leahy, *I Was There: The Personal Story of the Chief of Staff to Presidents Roosevelt and Truman, Based on His Notes and Diaries Made at the Time* (New York, 1950), p. 5.

10. Gar Alperovitz is the pathbreaker in the Cold War interpretation of Hiroshima — what he calls "atomic diplomacy." His book *Atomic Diplomacy: Hiroshima and Potsdam: The Use of the Atomic Bomb and the American Confrontation with Soviet Power* (New York, 1985) was first published in 1965. Alperovitz opened the way for other revisionist historians. The most important among them is Martin J. Sherwin,

A World Destroyed: Hiroshima and the Origins of the Arms Race (New York, 1987). Sherwin's book contains a very useful appendix with top secret military documents from the National Archives. "Russia(n)" was the term policymakers often used at the time.

11. Margaret Truman, Harry S. Truman (New York, 1973), p. 232.

12. Truman, Memoirs, p. 87.

13. Henry Stimson, Memorandum for the President, September 11, 1945, Stimson Diary, Yale University Archives; see also Stimson Diary, May 10 and 13, 1945; July 25, 1945.

14. Len Giovannitti and Fred Freed, The Decision to Drop the Bomb (New York, 1965), pp. 65–6.

15. Groves, testimony, U.S. Atomic Energy Commission, In the Matter of J. Robert Oppenheimer: Transcript of Hearing before Personnel Security Board (Cambridge, Mass., 1971), p. 173.

16. See Ronald Takaki, Iron Cages: Race and Culture in Nineteenth-Century America (New York, 1979); also Winthrop Jordan, White Over Black: American Attitudes toward the Negro, 1550–1812 (Chapel Hill, 1968).

17. See Ronald Takaki, Strangers from a Different Shore: A History of Asian Americans (Boston, 1989).

18. Studs Terkel, "The Good War": An Oral History of World War Two (New York, 1991), pp. 107–8.

19. William Hipple, "New Year's Report on the Pacific," Newsweek, vol. 25, Jan. 1, 1945, p. 28.

20. C. Wright Mills, The Sociological Imagination (New York, 1976).

21. Stimson, "The Decision to Use the Atomic Bomb," p. 97.

22. Merle Miller, Plain Speaking: An Oral Biography of Harry S. Truman (New York, 1986), p. 14. David McCullough's Truman (New York, 1992) is the best and most valuable biography.

23. Truman to Mary, 1948, reprinted in M. Truman, Truman, p. 5.

24. Truman, Memoirs, p. 419.

25. Lillian Hellman, quoted in Janet Landman, Regret: The Persistence of the Possible (New York, 1993), p. 8.

26. William Faulkner, quoted in Landman, Regret, p. 17.

27. For the "mirror" metaphor, see Barbara Tuchman, A Distant Mirror: The Calamitous Fourteenth Century (New York, 1978); Carlos Fuentes, A Buried Mirror: Reflections on Spain and the New World (Boston, 1992); and Ronald Takaki, A Different Mirror: A History of Multicultural America (New York, 1993).

28. Paul Klee, quoted in Landman, *Regret*, p. xxv. "Even when regret puts us in touch with [our] 'worse selves,'" counsels psychologist Landman, "it contributes significantly to a comprehensive sense of integrity that comes of sustaining one's link with who one was, while also sustaining one's link with one's present better self. Regardless of how bad are the regretted matters, genuine regret signifies that you have standards of excellence, decency, morality, or ethics you still care about — a good thing in itself. In addition, remaining in connection with your better values through regret can further the purpose of moving you to behave differently if a similar situation should present itself in the future." See Landman, *Regret*, p. 26.

29. Truman, quoted in Landman, *Regret*, p. 9.

30. Miller, *Plain Speaking*, p. 13.

31. *The New York Times*, "The Smithsonian and the Bomb," September 5, 1994. See also *New York Times*, "Exhibit Plans on Hiroshima Stir a Debate," August 28, 1994; letter to the editor, "Why Hiroshima Still Haunts America's Psyche," *New York Times*, October 16, 1994; editorial, "Hijacking History," January 30, 1995; *USA Today*, "A-Bomb Exhibit Still Under Fire," December 6, 1994; Hugh Sidey, "War and Remembrance," *Time*, May 23, 1994, p. 64. See also the thoughtful little essay by James Gilbert, "Memorializing the Bomb," *Radical History Review*, number 34 (1986), pp. 101–4. Regarding the brochure on the bomb display in the National Museum of American History, Gilbert observes that it does "not indicate why President Harry Truman decided to use it." "[T]he missing factor — and actor — is decision, policy, and consequence." Historian John Dower states: "It's important to recognize how much of American memory is myth. For example, that we used the bomb simply to win the war and save Americans lives is the dominant myth." Dower, quoted in William Lanouette, "Why We Dropped the Bomb," in *Civilization: The Magazine of the Library of Congress*, January–February, 1995, p. 37.

CHAPTER 2.   "SEVERAL SUNS IN MIDDAY"

1. Mark Twain, *A Connecticut Yankee in King Arthur's Court* (New York, 1963; originally published in 1889), pp. 14–15.

2. The "colossal reality" of the atomic bomb is from Henry L. Stimson and McGeorge Bundy, *On Active Service in Peace and War* (New York, 1937), p. 637.

3. Truman liked to get together with men for drinks, or what he called

"libation." Robert H. Ferrell (ed.), *Off the Record: The Private Papers of Harry S. Truman* (New York, 1980), p. 42.

4. Margaret Truman (ed.), *Where the Buck Stops: The Personal and Private Writings of Harry S. Truman* (New York, 1989), p. 371.

5. David McCullough, *Truman* (New York, 1992), p. 341.

6. Robert H. Ferrell, *Harry S. Truman: A Life* (Columbia, Mo., 1994), p. 176.

7. Ferrell, *Off the Record*, p. 15.

8. Truman, *Where the Buck Stops*, p. 204.

9. Margaret Truman, *Harry S. Truman* (New York, 1972), p. 209; Ferrell, *Off the Record*, p. 15; Truman, *Where the Buck Stops*, p. 372.

10. Merle Miller, *Plain Speaking: An Oral Biography of Harry S. Truman* (New York, 1986), p. 185.

11. Harry S. Truman, *Memoirs of Harry S. Truman: Year of Decisions, 1945* (New York, 1955), p. 10.

12. Truman, *Memoirs*, pp. 10–11; Stimson to Truman, March 13, 1944, Stimson Diary, Yale University Archives.

13. Telephone conversation between the secretary of war and Senator Truman, June 17, 1943, reprinted in Michael B. Stoff, Jonathan F. Fanton, and R. Hal Williams (eds.), *The Manhattan Project: A Documentary Introduction to the Atomic Age* (Philadelphia, 1991), p. 40.

14. Truman, *Memoirs*, pp. 10, 11.

15. Henry Stimson, Memorandum discussed with the President, April 25, 1945, Stimson Diary, Yale University Archives.

16. Leslie Groves, Memorandum for the Secretary of War, July 18, 1945, Manhattan Engineer District Records, National Archives.

17. M. Truman, *Truman*, p. 272.

18. Studs Terkel, *"The Good War": An Oral History of World War Two* (New York, 1984), p. 513.

19. I. I. Rabi, *Science: The Center of Culture* (New York, 1970), p. 138.

20. Peter Goodchild, *J. Robert Oppenheimer: Shatterer of Worlds* (Boston, 1981), p. 162.

21. Ferrell, *Off the Record*, p. 55.

22. Twain, *Connecticut Yankee*, p. 15.

23. Spencer Weart and Gertrud Weiss Szilard (eds.), *Leo Szilard: His Version of the Facts* (Cambridge, Mass., 1978), p. 17.

24. William Lanouette, *Genius in the Shadows: A Biography of Leo Szilard, The Man behind the Bomb* (Chicago, 1992), p. xvi.

25. Albert Einstein to F. D. Roosevelt, August 2, 1939, reprinted in Weart and Szilard, *Szilard*, pp. 94–6.

26. Lanouette, *Genius*, p. 210.

27. Twain, *Connecticut Yankee*, p. 14.

28. Martin Sherwin, *A World Destroyed: Hiroshima and the Origins of the Arms Race* (New York, 1987), p. 76.

29. Richard Rhodes, *The Making of the Atomic Bomb* (New York, 1986), pp. 402–5.

30. Stimson Diary, June 10, 1944 and December 13, 1944, Yale University Archives.

31. Leslie R. Groves, *Now It Can Be Told* (New York, 1962), p. 185.

32. Arthur H. Compton, *Atomic Quest: A Personal Narrative* (New York, 1956), pp. 222–3.

33. Groves, *Now It Can Be Told*, p. 184.

34. Weart and Szilard, *Szilard*, p. 181.

35. U.S. Atomic Energy Commission, *In the Matter of J. Robert Oppenheimer: Transcript of Hearing before Personnel Security Board* (Cambridge, Mass., 1971), pp. 32–3.

36. John Dower, "Science, Society, and the Japanese Atomic-Bomb Project During World War II," *Bulletin of Concerned Asian Scholars*, volume 10, no. 2 (April–June, 1978), p. 42. Rhodes agrees in *Atomic Bomb*: "Progress toward a Japanese atomic bomb, never rapid, slowed to frustration and futility across the middle years of the Pacific war." p. 580.

37. Groves, *Now It Can Be Told*, pp. 187, 141.

38. Grace Tully, *F.D.R., My Boss* (New York, 1949), p. 266.

39. Top Secret, "Tube Alloys," Aide-mémoire, September 18, 1944, Roosevelt and Churchill, reprinted in Stoff, et. al., *Manhattan*, p. 70; see also Stimson Diary, June 25, 1945, Yale University Archives.

40. V. Bush to Dr. Conant, September 23, 1944, reprinted in Stoff, et. al., *Manhattan*, pp. 74–5.

41. Scientists were confident the uranium-type bomb would explode; hence, they did not feel the need to test it. Sherwin states that bombing crews would be trained that year for a mission against Japan: "All these items Roosevelt approved." Sherwin, *World Destroyed*, p. 133. Barton J. Bernstein writes: "Though he never resolved how he would

use the bomb, Roosevelt jealously guarded his options." Later he adds: "Truman also inherited from Roosevelt the operating assumptions that the bomb was a legitimate weapon and that Japan was to be its target." Bernstein, "Doomsday II," *New York Times Magazine,* July 27, 1975, 21.

42. V. Bush and J. B. Conant, Memorandum to the Secretary of War, September 30, 1944, George Harrison–Harvey Bundy File, Folder 69, Manhattan Engineer District Records, National Archives.

43. Powaski, *Armageddon,* p. 13.

CHAPTER 3.   TO SAVE "HALF A MILLION" AMERICAN LIVES

1. John Hersey, *Hiroshima* (New York, 1959, originally published in 1946), pp. 114–5.

2. Harry S. Truman, *Memoirs of Harry S. Truman: Year of Decisions, 1945* (New York, 1955), p. 417. Martin Sherwin, in *A World Destroyed: Hiroshima and the Origins of the Arms Race* (New York, 1987), writes: "recently discovered estimates of invasion casualities dramatically contradict the figures released by Truman. . . ." p. xx. "The casualty estimates announced by Truman in the aftermath of Hiroshima were grossly exaggerated. . . ." p. xxii.

3. Truman, *Memoirs,* p. 417.

4. Extract from the Minutes of Meeting held at the White House, June 18, 1945, reprinted in appendix of Sherwin, *World Destroyed,* p. 362.

5. Sherwin, *World Destroyed,* p. xxii; Joint War Plans Committee, report of June 15, 1945, reprinted in ibid., appendix, p. 342.

6. Ibid., p. 349.

7. Ibid., p. 347.

8. Merle Miller, *Plain Speaking: An Oral Biography of Harry S. Truman* (New York, 1986), p. 51.

9. Minutes of Meeting at White House, June 18, 1945, reprinted in Sherwin, *World Destroyed,* appendix, pp. 357, 359.

10. Ibid., pp. 360–1, 362.

11. Margaret Truman (ed.), *Where the Buck Stops: The Personal and Private Writings of Harry S. Truman* (New York, 1989), p. 205.

12. Robert H. Ferrell (ed.), *Off the Record: The Private Papers of Harry S. Truman* (New York, 1980), p. 47.

13. Ronald Schaffer, *Wings of Judgment: American Bombing in World War II* (New York, 1985), p. 3.

14. Ibid., p. 26.

15. Ibid., p. 32.

16. Ibid., pp. 3, 36, 37.

17. Ibid., pp. 61, 62.

18. Studs Terkel, *"The Good War": An Oral History of World War Two* (New York, 1984), pp. 205, 353. Schaffer, in *Wings*, p. 97, estimates the conservative number of 35,000. David Irving, in *The Destruction of Dresden* (London, 1963), p. 210, estimates 83,000 to 135,000.

19. Thomas S. Power, *Design for Survival* (New York, 1964), p. 28.

20. John Dower, *War Without Mercy: Race and Power in the Pacific War* (New York, 1986), p. 41.

21. Curtis E. LeMay with McKinlay Kantor, *Mission with LeMay* (New York, 1965), p. 352; also Richard Rhodes, *The Making of the Atomic Bomb* (New York, 1986), p. 596.

22. Lee Kennett, *A History of Strategic Bombing* (New York, 1982), p. 176.

23. Schaffer, *Wings*, p. 142.

24. George E. Hopkins, "Bombing and the American Conscience During World War II," *The Historian*, vol. xxvii, no. 3, May 1966, p. 463.

25. "Atomic and Human Energy," *New Republic*, August 27, 1945, p. 240. Still, the editor added: "The eradication of Hiroshima is dramatic proof, not that we must or can fail to use the utmost destructive power available when we wage war, but rather that mankind can no longer afford to wage war." p. 241.

26. Mark Jonathan Harris, Franklin Mitchell, and Steven Schechter (eds.), *The Home Front: America During World War II* (New York, 1984), p. 210.

27. Joint War Plans Committee, report of June 15, 1945, reprinted in Sherwin, *World Destroyed*, appendix, p. 338.

28. Dwight D. Eisenhower, *Crusade in Europe* (Garden City, 1948), p. 443; Dwight D. Eisenhower, *The White House Years: Mandate for Change, 1953–56* (Garden City, 1963), pp. 312–3; see also Stimson Diary, July 20, 1945, Yale University Archives.

29. D. Clayton James, *The Years of MacArthur, 1941–1945*, vol. II, (Boston, 1975), p. 775. Had his opinion been requested before the issuance of the Potsdam Declaration's demand for an "unconditional surrender," MacArthur would have urged Truman to give the Japanese assurance that they could keep their emperor.

30. Lieutenant General Leslie R. Groves, interview transcript, October 20, 1969, p. 6, MacArthur Memorial Archive; Diller, interview transcript, "American Caesar," *Cineworld*, 9/26/82, p. 17, MacArthur Memorial Archive.

31. John P. Sunderland, "The Story Gen. Marshall Told Me," *U.S. News & World Report*, vol. 47, November 2, 1959, p. 52.

32. James, *MacArthur*, p. 773.

33. William D. Leahy, *I Was There: The Personal Story of the Chief of Staff to Presidents Roosevelt and Truman, Based on His Notes and Diaries Made at the Time* (New York, 1950), pp. 384–5, 259.

34. Ibid., p. 418.

35. Alperovitz, *Atomic Diplomacy*, p. 17.

36. Leahy, *I Was There*, p. 284.

37. U.S. Strategic Bombing Survey, *Japan's Struggle to End the War*, Washington, D.C., Government Printing Office, 1946, p. 13.

38. Leahy, *I Was There*, p. 385.

39. Alperovitz, *Atomic Diplomacy*, p. 28.

40. Ronald E. Powaski, *March to Armageddon: The United States and the Nuclear Arms Race, 1939 to the Present* (New York, 1987), p. 21.

41. James Byrnes, *Speaking Frankly* (New York, 1947), p. 211.

42. Truman, *Memoirs*, p. 396.

43. Leon V. Sigal, *Fighting to a Finish: The Politics of War Termination in the United States and Japan, 1945* (Ithaca, 1988), p. 90.

44. Robert E. Sherwood, *Roosevelt and Hopkins* (New York, 1950), p. 973.

45. Anne Armstrong, *Unconditional Surrender: The Impact of the Casablanca Policy upon World War II* (New Brunswick, N.J., 1961), p. 17.

46. Sigal, *Fighting*, p. 91.

47. Winston Churchill, *The Hinge of Fate* (Boston, 1950), p. 686.

48. Ibid., pp. 686–7; Richard Rhodes, *The Making of the Atomic Bomb* (New York, 1986), p. 521.

49. Sigal, *Fighting*, p. 91.

50. John Lewis Gaddis, *The United States and the Origins of the Cold War, 1941–1947* (New York, 1972), p. 9.

51. Truman, *Memoirs*, p. 207.

52. Winston Churchill, *Triumph and Tragedy* (Boston, 1953), p. 642.

53. Joseph C. Grew, *Turbulent Era: A Diplomatic Record of Forty Years, 1904–1945* (Boston, 1952), p. 1429.

54. Truman, *Memoirs*, p. 416.

55. Ibid., p. 417.

56. Minutes of Meeting at the White House, June 18, 1945, reprinted in Sherwin, *World Destroyed*, appendix, p. 361.

57. William Lanouette, "Why We Dropped the Bomb," *Civilization: The Magazine of the Library of Congress* (January–February, 1995), p. 34.

58. *Life*, "Japan, the Opportunity for Bringing Classic Statesmanship to Bear on Tokyo Still Exists," vol. 19, no. 6 (August 6, 1945), p. 24.

59. Stimson Diary, July 23 and 24, 1945, Yale University Archives.

60. Truman, *Memoirs*, p. 391.

61. Stimson, "The Decision to Use the Atomic Bomb," *Harper's Magazine*, vol. 194, no. 1161 (February 1947), p. 105.

62. Bertrand Goldschmidt, *Atomic Adventure* (New York, 1964), p. 35. See my discussion on the "corporate iron cage" in Ronald Takaki, *Iron Cages: Race and Culture in Nineteenth-Century America* (New York, 1979).

63. James F. Byrnes, Memorandum for the President, March 3, 1945, Harrison–Bundy File, Folder 2, Manhattan Engineer District Records, National Archives. See also Stimson Diary, February 18, 1944, Yale University Archives.

64. Notes of the Interim Committee Meeting, June 1, 1945, Harrison–Bundy File, Folder 100, Manhattan Engineer District Records, National Archives. Max Weber's "Bureaucracy," in H. H. Gerth and C. Wright Mills (eds.), *From Max Weber: Essays in Sociology* (New York, 1973), pp. 196–244, has influenced my conceptualization of the Manhattan Project's bureaucracy.

65. James F. Byrnes, Memorandum for the President, March 3, 1945, Harrison–Bundy File, Folder 2, Manhattan Engineer District Records, National Archives.

66. Major J. A. Derry and Dr. N. F. Ramsey, Memorandum for Major General L. R. Groves, May 12, 1945, reprinted in Michael B. Stoff, Jonathan F. Fanton, and R. Hal Williams (eds.), *The Manhattan Project* (Philadelphia, 1991), pp. 97–103.

67. Arthur Holly Compton, *Atomic Quest: A Personal Narrative* (New York, 1956), pp. 238–9. For the organizing of the committee, see Stimson Diary, May 2, 3, 1945, Yale University Archives.

68. Notes of the Interim Committee Meeting, May 31, 1945, National Archives.

69. Byrnes, *Speaking Frankly*, p. 261. See also Stimson Diary, May 8, 1945; June 1, 1945, Yale University Archives.

70. L. R. Groves, Memorandum for the Secretary of War, July 18, 1945, Manhattan Engineer District Records, National Archives.

71. Leslie R. Groves, *Now It Can Be Told* (New York, 1962), p. 265.

72. Schaffer, *Wings*, p. 173.

73. Ferrell, *Off the Record*, p. 55.

74. Truman, *Memoirs*, p. 419.

75. Stimson Diary, June 6, 1945, Yale University Archives.

76. Groves, *Now It Can Be Told*, p. 267.

77. Paul Boyer, *By the Bomb's Early Light: American Thought and Culture at the Dawn of the Atomic Age* (Chapel Hill, 1985), p. 232.

78. Log, reprinted in Groves, *Now It Can Be Told*, p. 318.

79. Paul W. Tibbets, Jr., as told to Wesley Price, "How to Drop an Atom Bomb," *Saturday Evening Post*, June 8, 1946, p. 136.

80. Francis Sill Wickware, "Manhattan Project," *Life*, vol. 19, no. 8, August 20, 1945, p. 111.

81. Len Giovannitti and Fred Freed, *The Decision to Drop the Bomb* (New York, 1965), p. 260.

82. Jim Garrison, *The Plutonium Culture: From Hiroshima to Harrisburg* (New York, 1980), p. 25; see also Powaski, *Armageddon*, p. 26.

83. Joseph Marx, *Seven Hours to Zero* (New York, 1967), p. 171; Rhodes, *Atomic Bomb*, p. 711.

84. Committee for "Children of Hiroshima," *Children of Hiroshima* (Cambridge, Mass., 1980), p. 228.

85. Ibid., pp. 6–7.

86. *Life*, "Hiroshima: Atom Bomb No. 1 Obliterated It," vol. 19, no. 8, August 20, 1945, p. 26.

87. Committee for "Children of Hiroshima," *Children*, p. 60.

88. Ibid., p. 128.

89. Ibid., p. 176.

90. Ibid., p. 262.

91. Ibid., p. 258.

92. David McCullough, *Truman* (New York, 1992), p. 454.

93. Leahy, *I Was There*, p. 430. Sherwin called Truman's statement "vile." See *World Destroyed*, p. 221.

94. Truman, *Memoirs*, p. 422.

95. *New York Times,* August 7, 1945.

96. Giovannitti and Freed, *Decision,* p. 268.

97. Ferrell, *Off the Record,* p. 55; Arthur Holly Compton, *Atomic Quest: A Personal Narrative* (New York, 1956), p. 254.

98. William Burchett, *Shadows of Hiroshima* (London, 1983), p. 34.

99. Sherwin, *World Destroyed,* p. 234.

100. Leonard Mosley, *Marshall* (New York, 1982), p. 340; Rhodes, *Atomic Bomb,* pp. 736–7.

101. Barton J. Bernstein, "Doomsday II," *New York Times Magazine,* July 27, 1975, p. 28.

102. Bernstein, "Doomsday II," p. 28.

103. Margaret Truman, *Harry S. Truman* (New York, 1972), p. 284.

104. Robert J. C. Butow, *Japan's Decision to Surrender* (Stanford, 1954), p. 158.

105. Robertson, *Byrnes,* p. 434.

106. Leahy, *I Was There,* p. 434; see also Stimson Diary, August 10, 1945, Yale University Archives. Stimson described Leahy's position as "good plain horse-sense."

107. Ferrell, *Off the Record,* p. 61.

108. Stimson, "Use of the Atomic Bomb," *Harper's,* p. 105.

109. *Life,* "Victory Reports around the World," vol. 19, no. 8, August 20, 1945, pp. 38–38A.

110. *New York Times,* August 11, 1945.

111. Herbert Feis, *The Atomic Bomb and the End of World War II* (Princeton, 1966), p. 143.

112. Paul Fussell, "Hiroshima: A Soldier's View," *New Republic,* vol. 185, nos. 8 & 9, August 22 & 29, 1981, p. 29. In the September 23, 1981, issue of the *New Republic,* Michael Walzer criticized Fussell's view. Fussell replied: "I was saying that I was simultaneously horrified about the bombing of Hiroshima and forever happy because the event saved my life. . . . My object was to offer a soldier's view, to indicate the complex moral situation of knowing that one's life has been saved because others' have been most cruelly snuffed out." p. 14.

113. Harris, et. al., *Homefront,* pp. 208–9.

114. Terkel, *"Good War,"* p. 291.

115. Ibid., p. 55.

116. William M. Tuttle, Jr., *"Daddy's Gone to War: The Second World War in the Lives of America's Children* (New York, 1993), p. 214.

117. Truman, *Memoirs,* p. 437.

118. Truman to his mother, August 12, 1945, quoted in M. Truman, *Truman,* p. 284.

CHAPTER 4. THE "OVERRIDING CONCERN": TWO SCHOOLS OF THOUGHT

1. Robert Frost, *Complete Poems of Robert Frost, 1949* (New York, 1949), p. 569. For the significance of the coming Cold War as a factor in the atomic bomb decision, see Gar Alperovitz, *Atomic Diplomacy* (New York, 1985) and Martin J. Sherwin, *A World Destroyed* (New York, 1987).

2. Merle Miller, *Plain Speaking: An Oral Biography of Harry S. Truman* (New York, 1986), p. 217.

3. Ibid., p. 82.

4. William Leahy, *I Was There: The Personal Story of the Chief of Staff to Presidents Roosevelt and Truman, Based on His Notes and Diaries Made at the Time* (New York, 1950), pp. 315–6.

5. James F. Byrnes, *Speaking Frankly* (New York, 1947), pp. 31–2.

6. Leahy, *I Was There,* p. 406.

7. Truman, *Memoirs,* pp. 85, 23, 80.

8. Ibid., p. x.

9. Margaret Truman, *Harry S. Truman* (New York, 1972), p. 232.

10. Robert H. Ferrell (ed.), *Off the Record: The Private Papers of Harry S. Truman* (New York, 1982), pp. 17–8.

11. Ibid., pp. 22, 44.

12. Joseph C. Grew, *Turbulent Era: A Diplomatic Record of Forty Years, 1904–1945* (Boston, 1952), pp. 1445–6.

13. John Lewis Gaddis, *The United States and the Origins of the Cold War, 1941–1947* (New York, 1972), p. 213.

14. Minutes of Meeting held at the White House, June 18, 1945, reprinted in Sherwin, *A World Destroyed,* appendix, pp. 358, 361.

15. Stimson Diary, May 15, 1945, Yale University Archives.

16. Sherwin, *World Destroyed,* p. 191.

17. Stimson Diary, June 6, Yale University Archives.

18. Leslie R. Groves, *Now It Can Be Told* (New York, 1962), p. 292.

19. U.S. Atomic Energy Commission, *In the Matter of J. Robert Oppenheimer: Transcript of Hearing before Personnel Security Board* (Cambridge, Mass., 1971), p. 31.

20. Stimson Diary, May 15, 1945, Yale University Archives.

21. V. Bush and J. B. Conant, Memorandum to the Secretary of War, September 30, 1944, Harrison–Bundy File, Folder 69, Manhattan Engineer District Records, National Archives.

22. Stimson Diary, Dec. 31, 1944, Yale University Archives.

23. Stimson, "The Decision to Use the Atomic Bomb," *Harper's Magazine*, vol. 194, no. 1161 (February 1947), p. 99. Stimson Diary, March 15, 1945, Yale University Archives.

24. Stimson, "Memorandum Discussed with President Truman," April 25, 1945, Stimson Diary, Yale University Archives.

25. Ibid.

26. Ferrell, *Off the Record*, p. 25.

27. Stimson Diary, June 6, 1945, Yale University Archives.

28. Truman to Bess, July 25, 1945, reprinted in Robert H. Ferrell (ed.), *Dear Bess: The Letters from Harry to Bess Truman, 1910–1959* (New York, 1983), p. 521.

29. Truman, *Memoirs*, p. 412.

30. Ibid., p. 145.

31. George L. Harrison, Memorandum for the Secretary of War, June 26, 1945, Harrison–Bundy File, Folder 77, Manhattan Engineer District Records, National Archives; Stimson Diary, July 3, 1945, Yale University Archives.

32. Truman, *Memoirs*, p. 416.

33. David Holloway, *Stalin and the Bomb: The Soviet Union and Atomic Energy, 1939–1956* (New Haven, 1994), p. 117.

34. Ferrell, *Off the Record*. See editor's note, p. 54.

35. Holloway, *Stalin*, p. 117.

36. At Hyde Park in September 1944, Roosevelt and Churchill had signed a secret aide-mémoire of an agreement for the strict Anglo-American joint control of the bomb. They agreed that "the suggestion that the world should be informed regarding tube alloys [the British code name for the atomic bomb project], with a view to an international agreement regarding its control and use, is not accepted." See "Tube Alloys," September 18, 1944, reprinted in Michael B. Stoff, Jonathan F. Fanton, and R. Hal Williams (eds.), *The Manhattan Project* (Philadelphia, 1991), p. 70. Truman did not know about this understand-

ing, however, when he made his decision not to tell Stalin about the bomb or share atomic technology with the Russians. See Sherwin, *World Destroyed*, p. 144. However, Leahy stated after the bombing of Hiroshima: "Truman questioned me as to whether any agreement had been made between Roosevelt and Churchill to give the British access to all details on the manufacture of the bomb. I told him of my recollections of a long discussion at Hyde Park after the 1944 Quebec Conference, and that my understanding was that Roosevelt had agreed to release to our ally only information on industrial use of atomic energy." Leahy, *I Was There*, p. 433.

37. David Robertson, *Sly and Able: A Political Biography of James F. Byrnes* (New York, 1994), p. 311.

38. Ferrell, *Off the Record*, p. 49.

39. Holloway, *Stalin*, p. 121. Barton J. Bernstein states: "There were, in short, two targets: Japan and Russia." See Barton J. Bernstein, "Doomsday II," *New York Times Magazine*, July 27, 1975, p. 21.

40. Notes of the Interim Committee Meeting, May 31, 1945, Harrison–Bundy File, Folder 100, Manhattan Engineer District Records, National Archives.

41. Spencer R. Weart and Gertrud Weiss Szilard (eds.), *Leo Szilard: His Version of the Facts* (Cambridge, Mass., 1978), p. 184.

42. Truman, *Memoirs*, p. 87; Alperovitz, *Atomic Diplomacy*.

43. Ronald Schaffer, *Wings of Judgment: American Bombing in World War II* (New York, 1985), p. 96.

44. Arthur Holly Compton, *Atomic Quest: A Personal Narrative* (New York, 1956), p. 221.

45. Groves, testimony, in U.S. Atomic Energy Commission, *In the Matter of J. Robert Oppenheimer: Transcript of Hearing before Personnel Security Board* (Cambridge, Mass., 1971), p. 173.

46. Barton J. Bernstein, "The Atomic Bomb and American Foreign Policy: The Route to Hiroshima," in Bernstein (ed.), *The Atomic Bomb: The Critical Issues* (Boston, 1976), p. 113.

47. Weart and Szilard, *Szilard*, p. 185.

48. Oppenheimer, testimony, in U.S. Atomic Energy Commission, *Oppenheimer*, p. 34.

49. Sherwin, *World Destroyed*, p. 200.

50. Compton, *Atomic Quest*, pp. 241, 236.

51. E. Teller to Leo Szilard, July 2, 1945, reprinted in Weart and Szilard, *Szilard*, p. 209.

52. Giovannitti and Freed, *Decision*, p. 206; see also Stimson Diary, July 24, 1945, Yale University Archives.

53. Joseph C. Grew, *Turbulent Era: A Diplomatic Record of Forty Years, 1904–1945* (Boston, 1952), pp. 1445–6, 1458; see also Stimson Diary, July 25, 1945, Yale University Archives.

54. Stalin had revised this date to August 15. Apparently, as the reader can see, he had reason to move it back to the original date.

55. Holloway, *Stalin*, p. 125.

56. Leahy, *I Was There*, p. 318.

57. Holloway, *Stalin*, pp. 123–4.

58. Forrestal Diary, July 28, 1945, reprinted in Stoff, et. al., *Manhattan*, p. 217.

59. Byrnes, *Speaking Frankly*, p. 208.

60. Holloway, *Stalin*, p.127.

61. Lisle A. Rose, *Dubious Victory: The United States and the End of World War II* (Akron, Ohio, 1973), p. 361.

62. Holloway, *Stalin*, p. 129.

CHAPTER 5.   REMEMBERING PEARL HARBOR

1. Leslie Marmon Silko, *Ceremony* (New York, 1978), pp. 257–8. See my analysis of the "demonic iron cage" in Ronald Takaki, *Iron Cages: Race and Culture in Nineteenth-Century America* (New York, 1979).

2. John Lewis Gaddis, *The United States and the Origins of the Cold War, 1941–1947* (New York, 1972), p. 1.

3. William F. Halsey and Joseph Bryan, *Admiral Halsey's Story* (New York, 1947), p. 123.

4. John Dower, *War Without Mercy: Race and Power in the Pacific War* (New York, 1986), p. 36.

5. Joseph Stilwell to Mrs. Stilwell, March 1, 1942, reprinted in Theodore H. White, *The Stillwell Papers* (New York, 1948), p. 49.

6. William Hipple, "New Year's Report on the Pacific," in *Newsweek*, vol. 25, Jan. 1, 1945, p. 28.

7. Arthur Holly Compton, *Atomic Quest: A Personal Narrative* (New York, 1956), p. 243.

8. *Fortune*, vol. 32, no. 6, December, 1945, p. 305.

9. Robert J. Donovan, *Conflict and Crisis: The Presidency of Harry S. Truman, 1945–1948* (New York, 1977), p. 100.

10. Paul Boyer, *By the Bomb's Early Light: American Thought and Culture at the Dawn of the Atomic Age* (Chapel Hill, 1994), p. 13.

11. Dower, *War Without Mercy*.

12. Ronald Takaki, *Strangers from a Different Shore: A History of Asian Americans* (Boston, 1989), p. 377.

13. Dower, *War Without Mercy*, p. 217.

14. Ibid., pp. 242–5.

15. William M. Tuttle, Jr., *"Daddy's Gone to War": The Second World War in the Lives of America's Children* (New York, 1993), p. 172.

16. George E. Hopkins, "Bombing and the American Conscience during World War II," *The Historian*, vol. 28, no. 3 (May 1966), p. 470.

17. Studs Terkel, *"The Good War": An Oral History of World War Two* (New York, 1984), p. 107.

18. Mark Jonathan Harris, Franklin Mitchell, and Steven Schechter (eds.), *The Homefront: America during World War II* (New York, 1984), p. 87. For a study of the "Other," see Edward Said, *Orientalism* (New York, 1978).

19. Tuttle, *"Daddy's Gone to War,"* p. 173.

20. Dower, *War Without Mercy*, pp. 34, 161, 37, 85.

21. Terkel, *"Good War,"* pp. 58–9.

22. Richard Tregaski, *Guadalcanal Diary* (New York, 1942), p. 15.

23. Tregaski, *Guadalcanal Diary*, p. 16.

24. Terkel, *"Good War,"* p. 64.

25. Dower, *War Without Mercy*, p. 66.

26. Allen Nevins, "How We Felt About the War," in Jack Goodman (ed.), *While You Were Gone: A Report on Wartime Life in the United States* (New York, 1946), p. 13.

27. Craig M. Cameron, *American Samurai: Myth, Imagination, and the Conduct of Battle in the First Marine Division, 1941–1951* (New York, 1994), pp. 98, 127.

28. Dower, *War Without Mercy*, p. 152; Cameron, *American Samurai*, p. 117.

29. Milton A. Hill, "The Lessons of Bataan," *Science Digest*, December 1942, p. 54.

30. James M. Merrill, *A Sailor's Admiral: A Biography of William F. Halsey* (New York, 1976), p. 111.

31. Ronald Takaki, *A Different Mirror: A History of Multicultural America* (New York, 1993), pp. 35, 36, 41, 43–4, 42.

32. Thomas Jefferson, *Notes on the State of Virginia* (New York, 1963, written in 1781), pp. 138–9; see also Ronald Takaki, *Iron Cages: Race and Culture in Nineteenth-Century America* (New York, 1979), pp. 36–66.

33. Jefferson to John Holmes, April 22, 1820, and to Jared Sparks, February 4, 1824, in Paul L. Ford (ed.), *The Works of Thomas Jefferson,* (New York, 1892–99), vol. 13, p. 159, and vol. 12, p. 334–9.

34. Jefferson to James Monroe, November 24, 1801, in Ford, *Works of Jefferson,* vol. 9, p. 317.

35. *Debates and Proceedings in the Congress of the United States, 1789–1791* (Washington, D.C., 1834), vol. 1, pp. 998, 1284; vol. 2, pp. 1148–56, 2264.

36. Jefferson to Uriah Forrest, December 31, 1787, in Julian Boyd (ed.), *The Papers of Thomas Jefferson* (Princeton, 1950–65), vol. 12, p. 487; Jefferson, *Notes on the State of Virginia,* pp. 157–8.

37. Frederick Jackson Turner, "The Significance of the Frontier in American History," in Turner, *The Early Writings of Frederick Jackson Turner* (Madison, 1938), pp. 185–96.

38. *San Francisco Alta,* June 4, 1853; *Hutching's California Magazine,* vol. 1 (March 1857), p. 387; *New York Times,* December 26, 1873; *The Wasp Magazine,* vol. 30 (January–June 1893), pp. 10– 11; *Report of the Joint Special Committee to Investigate Chinese Immigration,* Senate Report No. 689, 44th Congress, 2nd session, 1876–7, p. vi; Dan Caldwell, "The Negroization of the Chinese Stereotype in California," *Southern California Quarterly,* vol. 53 (June 1971), pp. 123–31. See also Alexander Saxton, *The Indispensable Enemy: Labor and the Anti-Chinese Movement in California* (Berkeley, 1971).

39. California Supreme Court, *The People v. Hall,* October 1, 1854, in Robert F. Heizer and Alan F. Almquist, *The Other Californians* (Berkeley, 1971), p. 229.

40. Letter from Saum Song Bo, *American Missionary* (October, 1885), reprinted in *East/West,* June 26, 1986. See also Takaki, *Strangers from a Different Shore,* p. 77.

41. Jacobus tenBroek, Edward N. Barnhart, and Floyd W. Matson, *Prejudice, War and the Constitution: Causes and Consequences of the Evacuation of Japanese Americans in World War II* (Berkeley, 1954), p. 19.

42. tenBroek, et al., *Prejudice,* p. 19.

43. Kazuo Ito, *Issei: A History of Japanese Immigrants in North America* (Seattle, 1973), pp. 93, 95, 99, 129.

44. Shiki Ito, "My Sixty-Four Years in America," in East Bay Japanese For

Action (ed.), *Our Recollections* (Berkeley, Calif., 1986), p. 125; "Life History of Sakoe Tsuboi," p. 3, Survey of Race Relations, 1924, Stanford University, Hoover Institution Library.

45. Eileen Sunada Sarasohn (ed.), *The Issei: Portrait of a Pioneer, an Oral History* (Palo Alto, 1983), pp. 64, 67.

46. Ito, *Issei*, pp. 94, 96, 98, 127, 128, 133, 134, 135; Kiyoshi Kawakami, "How California Treats the Japanese," *The Independent*, vol. 74 (May 8, 1913), p. 1020.

47. American Federation of Labor, *Proceedings* (1904), p. 100; Augusta Pio, "Exclude Japanese Labor," *American Federationist*, vol. 12, no. 3 (March 1905), pp. 275–6.

48. Yamato Ichihashi, *Japanese in the United States: A Critical Study of the Problems of the Japanese Immigrants and Their Children* (Stanford, 1932), p. 231; "Asiatic Exclusion League of North America, Preamble and Constitution, 1905," reprinted in appendix, Eliot Mears, *Resident Orientals on the American Pacific Coast* (New York, 1927), p. 435; Roger Daniels, *The Politics of Prejudice: The Anti-Japanese Movement in California and the Struggle for Japanese Exclusion* (New York, 1968), p. 85.

49. Ichihashi, Japanese, p. 236.

50. Ibid., p. 244; "The Gentlemen's Agreement," from *Report of Commissioner General of Immigration*, reprinted in appendix, Mears, *Oriental*, p. 443.

51. *California Statutes*, 1913, chapter 113.

52. In 1850, Hikozo, a shipwrecked fisherman from Japan, arrived in San Francisco and became an American citizen. The 1910 census showed 420 Japanese-born American citizens. See Bradford Smith, *Americans From Japan* (New York, 1948), p. 148.

53. Yuji Ichioka, "Early Japanese Immigrant Quest for Citizenship: The Background of the 1922 Ozawa Case," *Amerasia*, vol. 4, no. 2 (1977), pp. 10, 11, 17; Ichihashi, *Japanese*, p. 298; *Ozawa vs. United States, Decision of the Court*, November 13, 1922, reprinted in appendix, Mears, *Oriental*, pp. 509, 513, 514.

54. Section 13 of the 1924 Immigration Act, reprinted in appendix of Mears, *Oriental*, p. 515; "Life History and Social Document of Andrew Kan," August 22, 1924, pp. 12–13, Survey of Race Relations, Stanford University, Hoover Institution Library; Ichihashi, *Japanese*, p. 303.

55. "Message from Japan to America," the *Japan Times and Mail*, October 1, 1924, reprinted in appendix, Mears, *Oriental*, pp. 516–18.

56. Yuji Ichioka, *The Issei: The World of the First Generation Japanese Immigrants, 1885–1924* (New York, 1988), p. 247.

57. Ichihashi, *Japanese*, p. 312.

58. tenBroek, *Prejudice*, p. 26.

59. Dower, *War Without Mercy*, p. 157.

60. Homer Lea, *Valor of Ignorance* (New York, 1909); see also Daniels, *Politics of Prejudice*, pp. 72–3.

61. Daniels, *Politics of Prejudice*, p. 72.

62. Dower, *War Without Mercy*, pp. 158, 344.

63. Stimson Diary, February 10, 1942, Yale University Archives.

64. Ibid.

65. Robert A. Wilson and Bill Hosokawa, *East to America: A History of the Japanese in the United States* (New York, 1980), p. 154; Commission on Wartime Relocation and Internment of Civilians, *Personal Justice Denied* (Washington, D.C., 1982), p. 264.

66. Commission on Wartime Relocation, *Justice*, pp. 52–3.

67. Ibid., p. 55.

68. Roger Daniels, *Concentration Camps USA: Japanese Americans and World War II* (New York, 1971), pp. 45–6.

69. Commission on Wartime Relocation, *Justice*, p. 66.

70. Ibid., pp. 64, 73.

71. Ibid., pp. 56, 71.

72. Gary Y. Okihiro and Julie Sly, "The Press, Japanese Americans, and the Concentration Camps," *Phylon*, vol. XLIV, no. 1 (1983), pp. 66–9; tenBroek, *Prejudice*, p. 75.

73. Daniels, *Concentration Camps*, p. 62.

74. tenBroek, *Prejudice*, pp. 79–80.

75. Ibid., p. 80.

76. Ibid., p. 83.

77. Commission on Wartime Relocation, *Justice*, pp. 75, 78.

78. Ibid., pp. 78, 79.

79. Daniels, *Concentration Camps*, p. 65; Commission on Wartime Relocation, *Justice*, p. 66.

80. Congressman Robert Matsui, speech in the House of Representatives on the 442 bill for redress and reparations, September 17, 1987, *Congressional Record* (Washington, D.C., 1987), p. 7584.

81. Letter by Congressman Norman Mineta's father, quoted in the con-

gressman's speech to the House of Representatives, September 17, 1987, *Congressional Record* (Washington, D.C., 1987), p. 7585.

82. Commission on Wartime Relocation, *Justice,* p. 135.

83. Takaki, *Strangers from a Different Shore,* p. 19.

84. Ito, *Issei,* pp. 491, 429.

85. Jiro Nakano and Kay Nakano (eds. and trans.), *Poets Behind Barbed Wire* (Honolulu, 1983), p. 64.

86. Shig Doi, interview, in John Tateishi, *And Justice For All: An Oral History of the Japanese American Detention Camps* (New York, 1984), p. 161.

87. Andrew Lind, *Hawaii's Japanese: An Experiment in Democracy* (Princeton, 1946), pp. 161–2.

88. The philosopher in this case was Karl Marx. He was referring to economic circumstances. "Circumstances" in my chapter were cultural. See Marx, "Theses on Feuerbach," reprinted in Lewis S. Feuer (ed.), *Marx and Engels: Basic Writings on Politics and Philosophy* (New York, 1959), p. 244; Marx, "The German Ideology," reprinted in Lloyd D. Easton and Kurt H. Guddat, *Writings of the Young Marx on Philosophy and Society* (New York, 1967), p. 432.

89. Truman to Bess, June 22, 1911, reprinted in Robert H. Ferrell (ed.), *Dear Bess: The Letters from Harry to Bess Truman, 1910–1959* (New York, 1983), p. 39.

90. Truman to Bess, May 17, 1911, reprinted in Ferrell, *Dear Bess,* p. 34.

91. Merle Miller, *Plain Speaking: An Oral Biography of Harry S. Truman* (New York, 1986), p. 59.

92. Ibid., pp. 30, 44.

93. Harry S. Truman, *Memoirs of Harry S. Truman: Year of Decisions, 1945* (New York, 1955), p. 295.

94. Truman to Bess, August 4, 1939, reprinted in Ferrell, *Dear Bess,* p. 417.

95. David McCullough, *Truman* (New York, 1992), p. 54.

96. Truman to Bess, July 12, 1911, reprinted in Ferrell, *Dear Bess,* p. 41.

97. Truman to Bess, Nov. 22, 1911, reprinted in Ferrell, *Dear Bess,* p. 60.

98. Truman to Bess, March 23, 1912, reprinted in Ferrell, *Dear Bess,* p. 78.

99. Truman to Bess, August 9, 1930, reprinted in Ferrell, *Dear Bess,* p. 341.

100. Truman to Bess, July 17, 1935, reprinted in Ferrell, *Dear Bess,* p. 372.

101. Truman to Bess, January 6, 1936, reprinted in Ferrell, *Dear Bess*, p. 385.

102. Truman to Bess, September 15, 1940, reprinted in Ferrell, *Dear Bess*, p. 446.

103. Miller, *Plain Speaking*, pp. 222, 62, 195.

104. Robert J. Donovan, *Conflict and Crisis: The Presidency of Harry S. Truman, 1945–1948* (New York, 1977), p. 31.

105. Margaret Truman, *Harry S. Truman* (New York, 1972), p. 128.

106. Takaki, *A Different Mirror*, p. 400.

107. Margaret Truman (ed.), *Where the Buck Stops: The Personal and Private Writings of Harry S. Truman* (New York, 1989), p. 106.

108. Ibid., p. 15.

109. Miller, *Plain Speaking*, p. 452.

110. Ronald E. Powaski, *March to Armageddon: The United States and the Nuclear Arms Race, 1939 to the Present* (New York, 1987), p. 24.

111. Ferrell, *Off the Record*, pp. 53–6.

112. Boyer, *Bomb's Light*, p. 12.

113. Truman, quoted in Barton J. Bernstein, "The Atomic Bomb and American Foreign Policy: The Route to Hiroshima," reprinted in Bernstein (ed.), *The Atomic Bomb: The Critical Issues* (Boston: Little, Brown and Company, 1976), p. 113.

114. Ferrell, *Off the Record*, p. 53.

CHAPTER 6. WHERE THE BUCK STOPPED

1. Theodore Roosevelt, "The Strenuous Life," in Roosevelt, *The Strenuous Life: Essays and Addresses* (Philadelphia, 1903), pp. 10–11.

2. Merle Miller, *Plain Speaking: An Oral Biography of Harry S. Truman* (New York, 1986), p. 90.

3. Ibid., pp. 90–1.

4. Ibid., pp. 17, 108.

5. Truman to Bess, July 12, 1911, reprinted in Robert H. Ferrell (ed.), *Dear Bess: The Letters from Harry to Bess Truman, 1910–1959* (New York, 1983), p. 40.

6. Truman to Bess, June 29, 1949, reprinted in Ferrell, *Dear Bess*, p. 558.

7. Miller, *Plain Speaking*, pp. 83, 54.

8. Ibid., pp. 25, 65.

9. Ibid., p. 185.

10. *Time,* December 31, 1945, p. 16.

11. Miller, *Plain Speaking,* p. 181.

12. Ibid., p. 203.

13. Harry S. Truman, *Memoirs of Harry S. Truman: Year of Decisions, 1945* (New York, 1955), p. 5.

14. Robert H. Ferrell (ed.), *Off the Record: The Private Papers of Harry S. Truman* (New York, 1982), p. 16.

15. Truman to Mamma and Mary, reprinted in Truman, *Memoir,* p. 44.

16. Miller, *Plain Speaking,* p. 10. Margaret Truman reported that her father had been called the "accidental president." Margaret Truman, *Harry S. Truman* (New York, 1972), p. 43.

17. Truman, *Memoirs,* p. 5.

18. Miller, *Plain Speaking,* pp. 204–5.

19. M. Truman, *Truman,* p. 202.

20. Ferrell, *Off the Record,* p. 14.

21. Robert H. Ferrell, *Truman: A Life* (Columbia, Mo., 1994), p. 198.

22. Ferrell, *Off the Record,* p. 16.

23. Margaret Truman (ed.), *Where the Buck Stops: The Personal and Private Writings of Harry S. Truman* (New York, 1989), p. 372.

24. Miller, *Plain Speaking,* p. 34.

25. Miller, *Plain Speaking,* p. 206; see also Ferrell, *Off the Record,* p. 19.

26. Truman, *Where the Buck Stops,* p. 19.

27. Robert J. Donovan, *Conflict and Crisis: The Presidency of Harry S. Truman, 1945–1948* (New York, 1977), p. 15.

28. David McCullough, *Truman* (New York, 1992), p. 349.

29. M. Truman, *Truman,* p. 221.

30. Lisle A. Rose, *Dubious Victory: The United States and the End of World War II* (Akron, Ohio, 1973), p. 84.

31. Miller, *Plain Speaking,* pp. 206–7.

32. M. Truman, *Truman,* pp. 192, 58.

33. Truman, *Where the Buck Stops,* p. 78.

34. Ferrell, *Off the Record,* p. 16.

35. Stimson Diary, April 12 and 13, 1945, Yale University Archives.

36. William Leahy, *I Was There: The Personal Story of the Chief of Staff to Presidents Roosevelt and Truman, Based on His Notes and Diaries Made at the Time* (New York, 1950), pp. 345, 346.

37. Michael B. Stoff, Jonathan F. Fanton, and R. Hal Williams (eds.), *The*

Manhattan Project: A Documentary Introduction to the Atomic Age (Philadelphia, 1991), p. 7.

38. Alice Kimball Smith and Charles Weiner (eds.), *Robert Oppenheimer: Letters and Recollections* (Cambridge, Mass., 1980), p. 288.

39. Miller, *Plain Speaking,* p. 16, 155, 14.

40. John Lewis Gaddis, *The United States and the Origins of the Cold War, 1941–1947* (New York, 1972), p. 199.

41. Cabell Phillips, *The Truman Presidency: History of a Triumphant Succession* (New York, 1966), pp. 78–9.

42. Truman, *Memoirs,* p. 9.

43. Truman, *Where the Buck Stops,* p. 81, 10.

44. Truman, *Memoirs,* p. 116, 129. See my chapter "The Masculine Thrust Toward Asia," in Ronald Takaki, *Iron Cages: Race and Culture in Nineteenth-Century America* (New York, 1979), pp. 259–279.

45. Miller, *Plain Speaking,* pp. 50, 32–3.

46. Ibid., p. 19.

47. Ibid., p. 19.

48. McCullough, *Truman,* p. 43.

49. Truman to Bess, reprinted in Ferrell, *Dear Bess,* p. 80.

50. Miller, *Plain Speaking,* p. 74.

51. Ibid., p. 66.

52. Ibid., p. 66.

53. M. Truman, *Truman,* p. 51.

54. Miller, *Plain Speaking,* pp. 70, 71.

55. Ibid., pp. 19, 97.

56. Ibid., p. 88.

57. M. Truman, *Truman,* p. 59.

58. Miller, *Plain Speaking,* pp. 158, 86.

59. Truman, *Memoirs,* pp. 119–20.

60. Miller, *Plain Speaking,* p. 375.

61. Truman, *Memoirs,* p. 82.

62. Donovan, *Conflict and Crisis,* p. 53.

63. Rose, *Dubious Victory,* p. 317.

64. Truman, *Memoirs,* p. 86.

65. Ibid., p. 342.

66. M. Truman, *Truman*, p. 58; McCullough, *Truman*, p. 105, cites a military record showing Truman was five feet eight inches.

67. Ferrell, *Off the Record*, p. 53.

68. Leahy, *I Was There*, p. 431.

69. Stimson Diary, July 21 and 22, Yale University Archives. See Martin Sherwin, *Atomic Diplomacy* (New York, 1987), pp. 223–4, for Truman's toughness at Potsdam.

70. Stimson Diary, July 21 and 22, Yale University Archives.

71. Ibid.

72. Truman to Bess, July 20, 1945, reprinted in Ferrell, *Dear Bess*, p. 520.

73. Truman to Bess, July 25, 1945, Ibid., p. 521.

74. M. Truman, *Truman*, p. 269.

75. Ibid. pp. 269–70.

76. Henry L. Stimson and McGeorge Bundy, *On Active Service in Peace and War* (New York, 1948), p. 629.

77. Sherwin, *World Destroyed*, p. 172.

78. Truman, *Memoirs*, p. 50.

79. Ferrell, *Off the Record*, pp. 58, 53.

80. Truman, *Memoirs*, p. 35.

81. James F. Byrnes, *Speaking Frankly* (New York, 1947), p. 203.

82. Thomas G. Paterson, "Potsdam, the Atomic Bomb, and the Cold War: A Discussion with James Byrnes," *Pacific Historical Review*, vol. 41, no. 2 (May 1972), p. 228.

83. Stimson Diary, May 15, 1945, Yale University Archives.

84. Roosevelt, "The Strenuous Life," in Roosevelt, *The Strenuous Life*.

85. Stimson Diary, May 16, 1945, Yale University Archives. See also Sherwin, *World Destroyed*, pp. 191–2.

86. Ferrell, *Off the Record*, p. 31.

87. Martin Sherwin, *A World Destroyed* (New York, 1987), p. 59.

88. Robert Messer describes "bull bat time": "the end of the long working day when he [Byrnes] liked to relax over drinks with his office staff and unwind by thinking aloud about the day's events." See Messer, *The End of an Alliance: James F. Byrnes, Roosevelt, Truman, and the Origins of the Cold War* (Chapel Hill, 1992), pp. 105–6.

89. David Robertson, *Sly and Able: A Political Biography of James F. Byrnes* (New York, 1994), p. 421.

90. Henry L. Stimson, "The Decision To Use the Atomic Bomb," *Harper's Magazine*, vol. 194, no. 1161 (February 1947), p. 106.

91. Stimson Diary, May 14, 1945, Yale University Archives.

92. Stimson Diary, May 15, 1945, Yale University Archives.

93. Truman enjoyed playing poker with friends at night. In his diary on May 27, he wrote: "Went upstairs and found that Steve Early, Scott Lucas and Jack Nichols had arranged a poker game. They expected me to get into it. To be fair I announced that I'd leave at midnight because I didn't want to stay out after 1 a.m. and it would be that time when I 'hit the hay.'" See Ferrell, *Off the Record*, p. 37.

94. Ferrell, *Off the Record*, p. 49.

95. Donovan, *Crisis and Conflict*, p. 96.

96. *Santa Fe New Mexican*, "Atomic Bombs Drop on Japan," August 6, 1945, reprinted in Peter Goodchild, *J. Robert Oppenheimer: Shatterer of Worlds* (Boston, 1981), p. 6.

97. Gregg Herken, *The Winning Weapon: The Atomic Bomb in the Cold War, 1945–1950* (Princeton, 1981), p. 58.

98. Ferrell, *Truman*, p. 181. See my analysis of the "demonic iron cage" in Takaki, *Iron Cages*.

99. Miller, *Plain Speaking*, p. 62.

100. Groves, testimony, U.S. Atomic Energy Commission, *In the Matter of J. Robert Oppenheimer: Transcript of Hearing before Personnel Security Board* (Cambridge, Mass., 1971), p. 173.

101. Groves, *Now It Can Be Told*, p. 415.

102. Sherwin, *World Destroyed*, p. 227.

103. Messer, *End of Alliance*, p. 89.

104. Ibid., p. 128; see also Stimson Diary, August 12 to September 3, 1945, Yale University Archives.

105. U.S. Department of State, *Foreign Relations of the United States: Conferences at Washington and Quebec* (Washington, D.C., 1970), pp. 1117–18; see also Barton J. Bernstein, "Atomic Diplomacy and the Cold War," in Bernstein (ed.), *The Atomic Bomb: The Critical Issues* (Boston, 1976), p. 132.

106. Herken, *Winning Weapon*, p. 40.

107. *Time*, December 31, 1945.

CHAPTER 7. HIROSHIMA: FACES OF WAR AND HUMANITY

1. Leon V. Sigal, *Fighting to a Finish: The Politics of War Termination in the United States and Japan, 1945* (Ithaca, N.Y., 1988), p. 158.

2. Leslie R. Groves, *Now It Can Be Told* (New York, 1962), p. 324. Ronald Schaffer, *Wings of Judgment* (New York, 1985), pp. 149–76, chapter 8, "The Bombing of Japan: American Perceptions of the Moral Issue." Marshall felt the need to acknowledge what historian Ronald Schaffer called the moral issue of Hiroshima. In my chapter, I also examine this issue in relation to many of the key individuals involved in the dropping of the bomb. For a powerful portrait of the face of war and inhumanity, see José Clemente Orozco's mural at the Governor's Palace in Guadalajara, Mexico. Orozco invites us to "see" as he graphically unshrouds the pretenses and idealistic promises of nationalism, religion, and other ideologies that have led to violent conflicts.

3. Schaffer, *Wings*, p. 166.

4. Arthur Holly Compton, *Atomic Quest* (New York, 1956), p. 237.

5. Sigal, *Fighting*, pp. 131, 114.

6. John P. Sunderland, "The Story Gen. Marshall Told Me," *U.S. News & World Report*, November 2, 1959, p. 52.

7. William D. Leahy, *I Was There: The Personal Story of the Chief of Staff to Presidents Roosevelt and Truman, Based on His Notes and Diaries Made at the Time* (New York, 1950), pp. 441, 385, 434.

8. Ibid., pp. 440, 441.

9. Ibid., pp. 441–2.

10. Schaffer, *Wings*, p. 152.

11. Ibid., pp. 14, 102.

12. Ibid., p. 152.

13. Barton J. Bernstein, "Doomsday II," *New York Times Magazine*, July 27, 1975, p. 27.

14. Schaffer, *Wings*, p. 148.

15. Stimson Diary, April 23, 1945, Yale University Achives; William Shakespeare, *The Tempest*, act V, scene i.

16. Henry L. Stimson and McGeorge Bundy, *On Active Service in Peace and War* (New York, 1948), p. 637.

17. Stimson Diary, June 1 and 6, 1945, Yale University Archives.

18. Schaffer, *Wings*, pp. 99–100.

19. Stimson Diary, May 16, 1945, Yale University Archives.

20. Richard Rhodes, *The Making of the Atomic Bomb* (New York, 1986), p. 647.

21. Stimson, handwritten notes, May 31, 1945, reprinted in Rhodes, *Atomic Bomb*, p. 642.

22. Stimson, Memorandum for the President, July 2, 1945, reprinted in Stimson, "The Decision to Use the Atomic Bomb," *Harper's Magazine*, vol. 194, no. 1161 (February 1947), pp. 102–3; Stimson Diary, May 29, 1945; June 19, 1945, Yale University Archives.

23. Minutes of Meeting of the Committee of Three, June 12, 1945, Secretary of War's File, Records of the Office of the Secretary of War, Record Group 107, National Archives; Stimson and Bundy, *Active Service*, p. 629.

24. Stimson Diary, August 10, 1945, Yale University Archives.

25. Stimson Diary, January 9, 1943; July 18, 19, 23, 24, 1945, Yale University Archives.

26. Stimson Diary, December 31, 1944; Stimson, Memorandum discussed with the President, April 25, 1945, Stimson Diary, Yale University Archives.

27. Stimson Diary, September 17, 1945, Yale University Archives.

28. Stimson, Memorandum for the President, September 11, 1945, Stimson Diary, Yale University Archives.

29. Stimson, "The Decision to Use the Atomic Bomb," *Harper's*, pp. 98, 99, 103, 104.

30. Stimson and Bundy, *Active Service*, p. 633.

31. The Franck Report, June 11, 1945, reprinted in Stoff, et al., *Manhattan*, pp. 140–7.

32. George L. Harrison, Memorandum for the Secretary of War, June 26, 1945, Harrison–Bundy File, Folder 77, Manhattan Engineer District Records, National Archives.

33. Franck Report, in ibid., pp. 140–7.

34. Ibid.

35. Ibid.

36. Rhodes, *Atomic Bomb*, p. 637.

37. William Lanouette, *Genius in the Shadows: A Biography of Leo Szilard, The Man behind the Bomb* (Chicago, 1992), p. 260.

38. Ibid.

39. Leo Szilard, letter to accompany petition to Truman, July 4, 1945,

Harrison–Bundy File, Folder 71, Manhattan Engineer District Records, National Archives.

40. Lanouette, *Szilard,* p. 271.

41. Farrington Daniels to A. H. Compton, July 13, 1945, Harrison–Bundy File, Folder 71, Manhattan Engineer District Records, National Archives.

42. A Petition to the President of the United States, July 17, 1945, Harrison–Bundy File, Folder 71, Manhattan Engineer District Records, National Archives.

43. Lanouette, *Szilard,* pp. 276–7.

44. David Robertson, *Sly and Able: A Political Biography of James F. Byrnes* (New York, 1994), pp. 405–6.

45. Ronald W. Clark, *Einstein: The Life and Times* (New York, 1971), p. 554.

46. Terkel, *"Good War,"* p. 514.

47. Mark Jonathan Harris, Franklin Mitchell, and Steven Schechter (eds.), *The Homefront: America During World War II* (New York, 1984), p. 209.

48. Alice Kimball Smith and Charles Weiner (eds.), *Robert Oppenheimer: Letters and Recollections* (Cambridge, Mass., 1980), opening epigram.

49. Ibid., p. 253.

50. J. R. Oppenheimer, Recommendations on the Immediate Use of Nuclear Weapons, June 16, 1945, reprinted in Michael B. Stoff, Jonathan F. Fanton, and R. Hal Williams (eds.), *The Manhattan Project: A Documentary Introduction to the Atomic Age* (Philadelphia, 1991), pp. 149–53.

51. Rhodes, *Atomic Bomb,* pp. 734–5.

52. U.S. Atomic Energy Commission, *In the Matter of J. Robert Oppenheimer: Transcript of Hearing before Personnel Security Board* (Cambridge, Mass., 1971), p. 235.

53. John Hersey, *Hiroshima* (New York, 1959), pp. 114–5.

54. Smith and Weiner, *Oppenheimer,* pp. 310–11.

55. L. R. Groves, Memorandum for the Secretary of War, July 18, 1945, reprinted in Stoff, et. al., *Manhattan,* pp. 188–93.

56. Smith and Weiner, *Oppenheimer,* pp. 310–11.

57. Ibid., pp. 315–25.

58. Leslie Marmon Silko, *Ceremony* (New York, 1978), pp. 257–8.

59. Hanson W. Baldwin, "The Atomic Weapon," *New York Times,* August 7, 1945.

60. Hanson W. Baldwin, "The Atomic Bomb and Future War," *Life,* vol. 19, no. 8, August 20, 1945, pp. 17–20.

61. *Time,* "The Bomb," vol. 46, no. 8, August 20, 1945, p. 19.

62. *Life,* "The Atomic Age," vol. 19, no. 8, August 20, 1945, p. 32.

63. Boyer, *Bomb's Light,* p. 197.

64. Herbert Hoover, *Addresses upon the American Road* (New York, 1949), p. 14.

65. Terkel, *"Good War,"* p. 109.

66. Lisle A. Rose, *Dubious Victory: The United States and the End of World War II* (Akron, Ohio, 1973), p. 363.

67. *Time,* "Opinion," vol. 46, no. 8, August 20, 1945.

68. Rose, *Dubious Victory,* p. 363.

69. Walter G. Taylor, *Time,* vol. 46, no. 9, August 27, 1945, p. 2.

70. Ronald Takaki, *A Different Mirror: A History of Multicultural America* (New York, 1993), p. 399.

71. W. E. B. DuBois, "The Winds of Time: Negro's War Gains and Losses," *Chicago Defender,* September 15, 1945.

72. Hurston, quoted in Howard Zinn, *Declarations of Independence: Cross-Examining American Ideology* (New York, 1990), p. 100.

73. Rose, *Dubious Victory,* p. 240.

74. Truman, quoted in Janet Landman, *Regret: The Persistence of the Possible* (New York: Oxford, 1993), p. 9.

75. Merle Miller, *Plain Speaking: An Oral Biography of Harry S. Truman* (New York, 1974), pp. 13, 14, 66, 215, 216.

76. Groves, testimony, U.S. Atomic Energy Commission, *In the Matter of J. Robert Oppenheimer: Transcript of Hearing before Personnel Security Board* (Cambridge, Mass., 1971), p. 173.

77. Schaffer, *Wings,* p. 173; L. R. Groves, Memorandum for the Secretary of War, July 18, 1945, Manhattan Engineer District Records, National Archives.

78. Schaffer, *Wings,* p. 173.

79. David Robertson, *Sly and Able: A Political Biography of James F. Byrnes* (New York, 1994), p. 311.

80. Truman to Bess, January 6, 1936, reprinted in Robert H. Ferrell (ed.), *Dear Bess: The Letters from Harry to Bess Truman, 1910–1959* (New York, 1983), p. 385.

81. Robert H. Ferrell (ed.), *Off the Record: The Private Papers of Harry S. Truman* (New York, 1980), p. 49.

82. Abraham Lincoln, "The Gettysburg Address," reprinted in William Benton (publisher), *The Annals of America*, vol. 9 (Chicago, 1968), pp. 462–3.

83. Gunnar Myrdal, *An American Dilemma: The Negro Problem and Modern Democracy* (New York, 1962, originally published in 1944), pp. 1004, 1021.

84. Takaki, *Different Mirror*, p. 374; Chester Tanaka, *Go For Broke: A Pictorial History of the Japanese American 100th Infantry Battalion and the 442d Regimental Combat Team* (Richmond, Calif., 1982), p. 171.

85. Miller, *Plain Speaking*, pp. 44–6, 16.

86. Truman to Mamma and Mary, May 8, 1945, Truman, *Memoirs*, p. 206.

87. Miller, *Plain Speaking*, pp. 242–4.

88. Ibid., pp. 247–8.

89. Boyer, *Bomb's Light*, p. 193.

90. David McCullogh, *Truman* (New York, 1992), p. 475.

91. Boyer, *Bomb's Light*, p. 193.

92. Robert J. Donovan, *Conflict and Crisis: The Presidency of Harry S. Truman* (New York, 1977), p. 97.

93. Ibid., p. 100. Schaffer, *Wings*, p. 173, also points out Truman's "divided feelings about exploding nuclear weapons on enemy citizens." Alperovitz, on the other hand, states: "Finally, it is simply a fact of history that neither President Truman nor Secretary Byrnes appears to have experienced the moral difficulties with killing large numbers of civilians that so disturbed men like Eisenhower and Leahy." *Atomic Diplomacy*, p. 54.

94. Stimson Diary, August 9, 1945, Yale University Archives: "These two heavy blows have fallen in quick succession upon the Japanese and there will be quite a little space before we intend to drop another." Donovan, *Conflict and Crisis*, p. 98.

95. Henry A. Wallace, Diary, August 10, 1945, reprinted in Stoff, et al., *Manhattan*, p. 245.

96. McCullough, *Truman*, p. 460.

97. Ferrell, *Off the Record*, pp. 52–3.

98. Ibid.

99. Ibid., p. 53.

INDEX

Ronald Takaki is a leading internationally recognized scholar, a fellow of the Society of American Historians. A third-generation American, he holds a Ph.D. in history from the University of California, Berkeley, where he has been a professor of Ethnic Studies for over two decades. The Berkeley faculty has honored him with a Distinguished Teaching Award. He has lectured widely in the U.S., and has presented papers in Japan, Russia, Armenia, and South Africa. Takaki is the author of the critically acclaimed *Iron Cages: Race and Culture in Nineteenth-Century America* and the prize-winning *Strangers from a Different Shore: A History of Asian Americans* and *A Different Mirror: A History of Multicultural America.*

CPSIA information can be obtained
at www.ICGtesting.com
Printed in the USA
BVHW070057041221
622948BV00003B/107